MACBETH

William Shakespeare

SPARK PUBLISHING

Spark Publishing
A Division of Barnes & Noble
120 Fifth Avenue
New York, NY 10011
www.sparknotes.com

ISBN-13: 978-1-4114-0316-1
ISBN-10: 1-4114-0316-9

Please submit changes or report errors to www.sparknotes.com/errors.

Printed in the United States.

10 9 8 7 6 5 4 3 2 1

CONTENTS

CONTEXT

THE MOST INFLUENTIAL WRITER in all of English literature, William Shakespeare was born in 1564 to a successful middle-class glove-maker in Stratford-upon-Avon, England. Shakespeare attended grammar school, but his formal education proceeded no further. In 1582 he married an older woman, Anne Hathaway, and had three children with her. Around 1590 he left his family behind and traveled to London to work as an actor and playwright. Public and critical acclaim quickly followed, and Shakespeare eventually became the most popular playwright in England and part-owner of the Globe Theater. His career bridged the reigns of Elizabeth I (ruled 1558–1603) and James I (ruled 1603–1625), and he was a favorite of both monarchs. Indeed, James granted Shakespeare's company the greatest possible compliment by bestowing upon its members the title of King's Men. Wealthy and renowned, Shakespeare retired to Stratford and died in 1616 at the age of fifty-two. At the time of Shakespeare's death, literary luminaries such as Ben Jonson hailed his works as timeless.

Shakespeare's works were collected and printed in various editions in the century following his death, and by the early eighteenth century his reputation as the greatest poet ever to write in English was well established. The unprecedented admiration garnered by his works led to a fierce curiosity about Shakespeare's life, but the dearth of biographical information has left many details of Shakespeare's personal history shrouded in mystery. Some people have concluded from this fact and from Shakespeare's modest education that Shakespeare's plays were actually written by someone else—Francis Bacon and the Earl of Oxford are the two most popular candidates—but the support for this claim is overwhelmingly circumstantial, and the theory is not taken seriously by many scholars.

In the absence of credible evidence to the contrary, Shakespeare must be viewed as the author of the thirty-seven plays and 154 sonnets that bear his name. The legacy of this body of work is immense. A number of Shakespeare's plays seem to have transcended even the category of brilliance, becoming so influential as to affect profoundly the course of Western literature and culture ever after.

Shakespeare's shortest and bloodiest tragedy, *Macbeth* tells the story of a brave Scottish general (Macbeth) who receives a prophecy from a trio of sinister witches that one day he will become King of Scotland. Consumed with ambitious thoughts and spurred to action by his wife, Macbeth murders King Duncan and seizes the throne for himself. He begins his reign racked with guilt and fear and soon becomes a tyrannical ruler, as he is forced to commit more and more murders to protect himself from enmity and suspicion. The blood-bath swiftly propels Macbeth and Lady Macbeth to arrogance, madness, and death.

Macbeth was most likely written in 1606, early in the reign of James I, who had been James VI of Scotland before he succeeded to the English throne in 1603. James was a patron of Shakespeare's acting company, and of all the plays Shakespeare wrote under James's reign, *Macbeth* most clearly reflects the playwright's close relationship with the sovereign. In focusing on Macbeth, a fig-ure from Scottish history, Shakespeare paid homage to his king's Scottish lineage. Additionally, the witches' prophecy that Banquo will found a line of kings is a clear nod to James's family's claim to have descended from the historical Banquo. In a larger sense, the theme of bad versus good kingship, embodied by Macbeth and Duncan, respectively, would have resonated at the royal court, where James was busy developing his English version of the theory of divine right.

Macbeth is not Shakespeare's most complex play, but it is cer-tainly one of his most powerful and emotionally intense. Whereas Shakespeare's other major tragedies, such as *Hamlet* and *Othello*, fastidiously explore the intellectual predicaments faced by their subjects and the fine nuances of their subjects' characters, *Macbeth* tumbles madly from its opening to its conclusion. It is a sharp, jagged sketch of theme and character; as such, it has shocked and fascinated audiences for nearly four hundred years.

PLOT OVERVIEW

THE PLAY BEGINS with the brief appearance of a trio of witches and then moves to a military camp, where the Scottish King Duncan hears the news that his generals, Macbeth and Banquo, have defeated two separate invading armies—one from Ireland, led by the rebel Macdonald, and one from Norway. Following their pitched battle with these enemy forces, Macbeth and Banquo encounter the witches as they cross a moor. The witches prophesy that Macbeth will be made thane (a rank of Scottish nobility) of Cawdor and eventually King of Scotland. They also prophesy that Macbeth's companion, Banquo, will beget a line of Scottish kings, although Banquo will never be king himself. The witches vanish, and Macbeth and Banquo treat their prophecies skeptically until some of King Duncan's men come to thank the two generals for their victories in battle and to tell Macbeth that he has indeed been named thane of Cawdor. The previous thane betrayed Scotland by fighting for the Norwegians and Duncan has condemned him to death. Macbeth is intrigued by the possibility that the remainder of the witches' prophecy—that he will be crowned king—might be true, but he is uncertain what to expect. He visits with King Duncan, and they plan to dine together at Inverness, Macbeth's castle, that night. Macbeth writes ahead to his wife, Lady Macbeth, telling her all that has happened.

Lady Macbeth suffers none of her husband's uncertainty. She desires the kingship for him and wants him to murder Duncan in order to obtain it. When Macbeth arrives at Inverness, she overrides all of her husband's objections and persuades him to kill the king that very night. He and Lady Macbeth plan to get Duncan's two chamberlains drunk so they will black out; the next morning they will blame the murder on the chamberlains, who will be defenseless, as they will remember nothing. While Duncan is asleep, Macbeth stabs him, despite his doubts and a number of supernatural portents, including a vision of a bloody dagger. When Duncan's death is discovered the next morning, Macbeth kills the chamberlains—ostensibly out of rage at their crime—and easily assumes the kingship. Duncan's sons Malcolm and Donalbain flee to England and Ireland, respectively, fearing that whoever killed Duncan desires their demise as well.

Fearful of the witches' prophecy that Banquo's heirs will seize the throne, Macbeth hires a group of murderers to kill Banquo and his son Fleance. They ambush Banquo on his way to a royal feast, but they fail to kill Fleance, who escapes into the night. Macbeth becomes furious: as long as Fleance is alive, he fears that his power remains insecure. At the feast that night, Banquo's ghost visits Macbeth. When he sees the ghost, Macbeth raves fearfully, startling his guests, who include most of the great Scottish nobility. Lady Macbeth tries to neutralize the damage, but Macbeth's kingship incites increasing resistance from his nobles and subjects. Frightened, Macbeth goes to visit the witches in their cavern. There, they show him a sequence of demons and spirits who present him with further prophecies: he must beware of Macduff, a Scottish nobleman who opposed Macbeth's accession to the throne; he is incapable of being harmed by any man born of woman; and he will be safe until Birnam Wood comes to Dunsinane Castle. Macbeth is relieved and feels secure, because he knows that all men are born of women and that forests cannot move. When he learns that Macduff has fled to England to join Malcolm, Macbeth orders that Macduff's castle be seized and, most cruelly, that Lady Macduff and her children be murdered.

When news of his family's execution reaches Macduff in England, he is stricken with grief and vows revenge. Prince Malcolm, Duncan's son, has succeeded in raising an army in England, and Macduff joins him as he rides to Scotland to challenge Macbeth's forces. The invasion has the support of the Scottish nobles, who are appalled and frightened by Macbeth's tyrannical and murderous behavior. Lady Macbeth, meanwhile, becomes plagued with fits of sleepwalking in which she bemoans what she believes to be bloodstains on her hands. Before Macbeth's opponents arrive, Macbeth receives news that she has killed herself, causing him to sink into a deep and pessimistic despair. Nevertheless, he awaits the English and fortifies Dunsinane, to which he seems to have withdrawn in order to defend himself, certain that the witches' prophecies guarantee his invincibility. He is struck numb with fear, however, when he learns that the English army is advancing on Dunsinane shielded with boughs cut from Birnam Wood. Birnam Wood is indeed coming to Dunsinane, fulfilling half of the witches' prophecy.

In the battle, Macbeth hews violently, but the English forces gradually overwhelm his army and castle. On the battlefield, Macbeth encounters the vengeful Macduff, who declares that he was not "of woman born" but was instead "untimely ripped" from his mother's womb (what we now call birth by cesarean section). Though he realizes that he is doomed, Macbeth continues to fight until Macduff kills and beheads him. Malcolm, now the King of Scotland, declares his benevolent intentions for the country and invites all to see him crowned at Scone.

CHARACTER LIST

Macbeth   Macbeth is a Scottish general and the thane of Glamis who is led to wicked thoughts by the prophecies of the three witches, especially after their prophecy that he will be made thane of Cawdor comes true. Macbeth is a brave soldier and a powerful man, but he is not a virtuous one. He is easily tempted into murder to fulfill his ambitions to the throne, and once he commits his first crime and is crowned King of Scotland, he embarks on further atrocities with increasing ease. Ultimately, Macbeth proves himself better suited to the battlefield than to political intrigue, because he lacks the skills necessary to rule without being a tyrant. His response to every problem is violence and murder. Unlike Shakespeare's great villains, such as Iago in *Othello* and Richard III in *Richard III,* Macbeth is never comfortable in his role as a criminal. He is unable to bear the psychological consequences of his atrocities.

Lady Macbeth Macbeth's wife, a deeply ambitious woman who lusts for power and position. Early in the play she seems to be the stronger and more ruthless of the two, as she urges her husband to kill Duncan and seize the crown. After the bloodshed begins, however, Lady Macbeth falls victim to guilt and madness to an even greater degree than her husband. Her conscience affects her to such an extent that she eventually commits suicide. Interestingly, she and Macbeth are presented as being deeply in love, and many of Lady Macbeth's speeches imply that her influence over her husband is primarily sexual. Their joint alienation from the world, occasioned by their partnership in crime, seems to strengthen the attachment that they feel to each another.

The Three Witches Three "black and midnight hags" who plot mischief against Macbeth using charms, spells, and prophecies. Their predictions prompt him to murder Duncan, to order the deaths of Banquo and his son, and to blindly believe in his own immortality. The play leaves the witches' true identity unclear—aside from the fact that they are servants of Hecate, we know little about their place in the cosmos. In some ways they resemble the mythological Fates, who impersonally weave the threads of human destiny. They clearly take a perverse delight in using their knowledge of the future to toy with and destroy human beings.

Banquo The brave, noble general whose children, according to the witches' prophecy, will inherit the Scottish throne. Like Macbeth, Banquo thinks ambitious thoughts, but he does not translate those thoughts into action. In a sense, Banquo's character stands as a rebuke to Macbeth, since he represents the path Macbeth chose not to take: a path in which ambition need not lead to betrayal and murder. Appropriately, then, it is Banquo's ghost—and not Duncan's—that haunts Macbeth. In addition to embodying Macbeth's guilt for killing Banquo, the ghost also reminds Macbeth that he did not emulate Banquo's reaction to the witches' prophecy.

King Duncan The good King of Scotland whom Macbeth, in his ambition for the crown, murders. Duncan is the model of a virtuous, benevolent, and farsighted ruler. His death symbolizes the destruction of an order in Scotland that can be restored only when Duncan's line, in the person of Malcolm, once more occupies the throne.

Macduff A Scottish nobleman hostile to Macbeth's kingship from the start. He eventually becomes a leader of the crusade to unseat Macbeth. The crusade's mission is to place the rightful king, Malcolm, on the throne, but Macduff also desires vengeance for Macbeth's murder of Macduff's wife and young son.

Malcolm   The son of Duncan, whose restoration to the throne signals Scotland's return to order following Macbeth's reign of terror. Malcolm becomes a serious challenge to Macbeth with Macduff's aid (and the support of England). Prior to this, he appears weak and uncertain of his own power, as when he and Donalbain flee Scotland after their father's murder.

Hecate   The goddess of witchcraft, who helps the three witches work their mischief on Macbeth.

Fleance   Banquo's son, who survives Macbeth's attempt to murder him. At the end of the play, Fleance's whereabouts are unknown. Presumably, he may come to rule Scotland, fulfilling the witches' prophecy that Banquo's sons will sit on the Scottish throne.

Lennox   A Scottish nobleman.

Ross   A Scottish nobleman.

The Murderers   A group of ruffians conscripted by Macbeth to murder Banquo, Fleance (whom they fail to kill), and Macduff's wife and children.

Porter   The drunken doorman of Macbeth's castle.

Lady Macduff   Macduff's wife. The scene in her castle provides our only glimpse of a domestic realm other than that of Macbeth and Lady Macbeth. She and her home serve as contrasts to Lady Macbeth and the hellish world of Inverness.

Donalbain   Duncan's son and Malcolm's younger brother.

ANALYSIS OF MAJOR CHARACTERS

MACBETH

Because we first hear of Macbeth in the wounded captain's account of his battlefield valor, our initial impression is of a brave and capable warrior. This perspective is complicated, however, once we see Macbeth interact with the three witches. We realize that his physical courage is joined by a consuming ambition and a tendency to self-doubt—the prediction that he will be king brings him joy, but it also creates inner turmoil. These three attributes—bravery, ambition, and self-doubt—struggle for mastery of Macbeth throughout the play. Shakespeare uses Macbeth to show the terrible effects that ambition and guilt can have on a man who lacks strength of character. We may classify Macbeth as irrevocably evil, but his weak character separates him from Shakespeare's great villains—Iago in *Othello*, Richard III in *Richard III*, Edmund in *King Lear*—who are all strong enough to conquer guilt and self-doubt. Macbeth, great warrior though he is, is ill equipped for the psychic consequences of crime.

Before he kills Duncan, Macbeth is plagued by worry and almost aborts the crime. It takes Lady Macbeth's steely sense of purpose to push him into the deed. After the murder, however, her powerful personality begins to disintegrate, leaving Macbeth increasingly alone. He fluctuates between fits of fevered action, in which he plots a series of murders to secure his throne, and moments of terrible guilt (as when Banquo's ghost appears) and absolute pessimism (after his wife's death, when he seems to succumb to despair). These fluctuations reflect the tragic tension within Macbeth: he is at once too ambitious to allow his conscience to stop him from murdering his way to the top and too conscientious to be happy with himself as a murderer. As things fall apart for him at the end of the play, he seems almost relieved—with the English army at his gates, he can finally return to life as a warrior, and he displays a kind of reckless bravado as his enemies surround him and drag him down. In part, this stems from his fatal confidence in the witches' prophecies, but it also seems to derive from the fact that he has returned to the arena where he has been most successful and where his internal turmoil need not affect him—namely, the battlefield. Unlike many of Shakespeare's other tragic heroes, Macbeth never seems to contemplate suicide: "Why should I play the Roman fool," he asks, "and die / On mine own sword?" (V.x.1–2). Instead, he goes down fighting, bringing the play full circle: it begins with Macbeth winning on the battlefield and ends with him dying in combat.

LADY MACBETH

Lady Macbeth is one of Shakespeare's most famous and frightening female characters. When we first see her, she is already plotting Duncan's murder, and she is stronger, more ruthless, and more ambitious than her husband. She seems fully aware of this and knows that she will have to push Macbeth into committing murder. At one point, she wishes that she were not a woman so that she could do it herself. This theme of the relationship between gender and power is key to Lady Macbeth's character: her husband implies that she is a masculine soul inhabiting a female body, which seems to link masculinity to ambition and violence. Shakespeare, however, seems to use her, and the witches, to undercut Macbeth's idea that "undaunted mettle should compose / Nothing but males" (I.vii.73–74). These crafty women use *female* methods of achieving power—that is, manipulation—to further their supposedly male ambitions. Women, the play implies, can be as ambitious and cruel as men, yet social constraints deny them the means to pursue these ambitions on their own.

Lady Macbeth manipulates her husband with remarkable effectiveness, overriding all his objections; when he hesitates to murder, she repeatedly questions his manhood until he feels that he must commit murder to prove himself. Lady Macbeth's remarkable strength of will persists through the murder of the king—it is she who steadies her husband's nerves immediately after the crime has been perpetrated. Afterward, however, she begins a slow slide into madness—just as ambition affects her more strongly than Macbeth before the crime, so does guilt plague her more strongly afterward. By the close of the play, she has been reduced to sleepwalking through the castle, desperately trying to wash away an invisible bloodstain. Once the sense of guilt comes home to roost, Lady Macbeth's sensitivity becomes a weakness, and she is unable to cope. Significantly, she (apparently) kills herself, signaling her total inability to deal with the legacy of their crimes.

THE THREE WITCHES

Throughout the play, the witches—referred to as the "weird sisters" by many of the characters—lurk like dark thoughts and unconscious temptations to evil. In part, the mischief they cause stems from their supernatural powers, but mainly it is the result of their understanding of the weaknesses of their specific interlocutors—they play upon Macbeth's ambition like puppeteers.

The witches' beards, bizarre potions, and rhymed speech make them seem slightly ridiculous, like caricatures of the supernatural. Shakespeare has them speak in rhyming couplets throughout (their most famous line is probably "Double, double, toil and trouble, / Fire burn and cauldron bubble" in IV.i.10–11), which separates them from the other characters, who mostly speak in blank verse. The witches' words seem almost comical, like malevolent nursery rhymes. Despite the absurdity of their "eye of newt and toe of frog" recipes, however, they are clearly the most dangerous characters in the play, being both tremendously powerful and utterly wicked (IV.i.14).

The audience is left to ask whether the witches are independent agents toying with human lives, or agents of fate, whose prophecies are only reports of the inevitable. The witches bear a striking and obviously intentional resemblance to the Fates, female characters in both Norse and Greek mythology who weave the fabric of human lives and then cut the threads to end them. Some of their prophecies seem self-fulfilling. For example, it is doubtful that Macbeth would have murdered his king without the push given by the witches' predictions. In other cases, though, their prophecies are just remarkably accurate readings of the future—it is hard to see Birnam Wood coming to Dunsinane as being self-fulfilling in any way. The play offers no easy answers. Instead, Shakespeare keeps the witches well outside the limits of human comprehension. They embody an unreasoning, instinctive evil.

THEMES, MOTIFS & SYMBOLS

THEMES

Themes are the fundamental and often universal ideas explored in a literary work.

THE CORRUPTING POWER OF UNCHECKED AMBITION

The main theme of *Macbeth*—the destruction wrought when ambition goes unchecked by moral constraints—finds its most powerful expression in the play's two main characters. Macbeth is a courageous Scottish general who is not naturally inclined to commit evil deeds, yet he deeply desires power and advancement. He kills Duncan against his better judgment and afterward stews in guilt and paranoia. Toward the end of the play he descends into a kind of frantic, boastful madness. Lady Macbeth, on the other hand, pursues her goals with greater determination, yet she is less capable of withstanding the repercussions of her immoral acts. One of Shakespeare's most forcefully drawn female characters, she spurs her husband mercilessly to kill Duncan and urges him to be strong in the murder's aftermath, but she is eventually driven to distraction by the effect of Macbeth's repeated bloodshed on her conscience. In each case, ambition—helped, of course, by the malign prophecies of the witches—is what drives the couple to ever more terrible atrocities. The problem, the play suggests, is that once one decides to use violence to further one's quest for power, it is difficult to stop. There are always potential threats to the throne—Banquo, Fleance, Macduff—and it is always tempting to use violent means to dispose of them.

THE RELATIONSHIP BETWEEN
CRUELTY AND MASCULINITY

Characters in *Macbeth* frequently dwell on issues of gender. Lady Macbeth manipulates her husband by questioning his manhood, wishes that she herself could be "unsexed," and does not contradict Macbeth when he says that a woman like her should give birth only to boys. In the same manner that Lady Macbeth goads her husband on to murder, Macbeth provokes the murderers he hires to kill Banquo by questioning their manhood. Such acts show that both Macbeth and Lady Macbeth equate masculinity with naked aggression, and whenever they converse about manhood, violence soon follows. Their understanding of manhood allows the political order depicted in the play to descend into chaos.

At the same time, however, the audience cannot help noticing that women are also sources of violence and evil. The witches' prophecies spark Macbeth's ambitions and then encourage his violent behavior; Lady Macbeth provides the brains and the will behind her husband's plotting; and the only divine being to appear is Hecate, the *goddess* of witchcraft. Arguably, *Macbeth* traces the root of chaos and evil to women, which has led some critics to argue that this is Shakespeare's most misogynistic play. While the male characters are just as violent and prone to evil as the women, the aggression of the female characters is more striking because it goes against prevailing expectations of how women ought to behave. Lady Macbeth's behavior certainly shows that women can be as ambitious and cruel as men. Whether because of the constraints of her society or because she is not fearless enough to kill, Lady Macbeth relies on deception and manipulation rather than violence to achieve her ends.

Ultimately, the play does put forth a revised and less destructive definition of manhood. In the scene where Macduff learns of the murders of his wife and child, Malcolm consoles him by encouraging him to take the news in "manly" fashion, by seeking revenge upon Macbeth. Macduff shows the young heir apparent that he has a mistaken understanding of masculinity. To Malcolm's suggestion, "Dispute it like a man," Macduff replies, "I shall do so. But I must also feel it as a man" (IV.iii.221–223). At the end of the play, Siward receives news of his son's death rather complacently. Malcolm responds: "He's worth more sorrow [than you have expressed] / And that I'll spend for him" (V.xi.16–17). Malcolm's comment shows that he has learned the lesson Macduff gave him on the sentient nature of true masculinity. It also suggests that, with Malcolm's coronation, order will be restored to the Kingdom of Scotland.

THE DIFFERENCE BETWEEN KINGSHIP AND TYRANNY

In the play, Duncan is always referred to as a "king," while Macbeth soon becomes known as the "tyrant." The difference between the two types of rulers seems to be expressed in a conversation that occurs in Act IV, scene iii, when Macduff meets Malcolm in

THEMES

England. In order to test Macduff's loyalty to Scotland, Malcolm pretends that he would make an even worse king than Macbeth. He tells Macduff of his reproachable qualities—among them a thirst for personal power and a violent temperament, both of which seem to characterize Macbeth perfectly. On the other hand, Malcolm says, "The king-becoming graces / [are] justice, verity, temp'rance, stableness, / Bounty, perseverance, mercy, [and] lowliness" (IV.iii.92–93). The model king, then, offers the kingdom an embodiment of order and justice, but also comfort and affection. Under him, subjects are rewarded according to their merits, as when Duncan makes Macbeth thane of Cawdor after Macbeth's victory over the invaders. Most important, the king must be loyal to Scotland above his own interests. Macbeth, by contrast, brings only chaos to Scotland—symbolized in the bad weather and bizarre supernatural events—and offers no real justice, only a habit of capriciously murdering those he sees as a threat. As the embodiment of tyranny, he must be overcome by Malcolm so that Scotland can have a true king once more.

Motifs

Motifs are recurring structures, contrasts, and literary devices that can help to develop and inform the text's major themes.

Hallucinations

Visions and hallucinations recur throughout the play and serve as reminders of Macbeth and Lady Macbeth's joint culpability for the growing body count. When he is about to kill Duncan, Macbeth sees a dagger floating in the air. Covered with blood and pointed toward the king's chamber, the dagger represents the bloody course on which Macbeth is about to embark. Later, he sees Banquo's ghost sitting in a chair at a feast, pricking his conscience by mutely reminding him that he murdered his former friend. The seemingly hardheaded Lady Macbeth also eventually gives way to visions, as she sleepwalks and believes that her hands are stained with blood that cannot be washed away by any amount of water. In each case, it is ambiguous whether the vision is real or purely hallucinatory; but, in both cases, the Macbeths read them uniformly as supernatural signs of their guilt.

VIOLENCE

Macbeth is a famously violent play. Interestingly, most of the killings take place offstage, but throughout the play the characters provide the audience with gory descriptions of the carnage, from the opening scene where the captain describes Macbeth and Banquo wading in blood on the battlefield, to the endless references to the blood-stained hands of Macbeth and his wife. The action is bookended by a pair of bloody battles: in the first, Macbeth defeats the invaders; in the second, he is slain and beheaded by Macduff. In between is a series of murders: Duncan, Duncan's chamberlains, Banquo, Lady Macduff, and Macduff's son all come to bloody ends. By the end of the action, blood seems to be everywhere.

PROPHECY

Prophecy sets *Macbeth*'s plot in motion—namely, the witches' prophecy that Macbeth will become first thane of Cawdor and then king. The weird sisters make a number of other prophecies: they tell us that Banquo's heirs will be kings, that Macbeth should beware Macduff, that Macbeth is safe till Birnam Wood comes to Dunsinane, and that no man born of woman can harm Macbeth. Save for the prophecy about Banquo's heirs, all of these predictions are fulfilled within the course of the play. Still, it is left deliberately ambiguous whether some of them are self-fulfilling—for example, whether Macbeth wills himself to be king or is fated to be king. Additionally, as the Birnam Wood and "born of woman" prophecies make clear, the prophecies must be interpreted as riddles, since they do not always mean what they seem to mean.

SYMBOLS

Symbols are objects, characters, figures, and colors used to represent abstract ideas or concepts.

BLOOD

Blood is everywhere in *Macbeth*, beginning with the opening battle between the Scots and the Norwegian invaders, which is described in harrowing terms by the wounded captain in Act I, scene ii. Once Macbeth and Lady Macbeth embark upon their murderous journey, blood comes to symbolize their guilt, and they begin to feel that their crimes have stained them in a way that cannot be washed clean. "Will all great Neptune's ocean wash this blood / Clean from my hand?" Macbeth cries after he has killed Duncan, even as his wife scolds him and says that a little water will do the job (II.ii.58–59). Later, though, she comes to share his horrified sense of being stained: "Out, damned spot; out, I say . . . who would have thought the old man to have had so much blood in him?" she asks as she wanders through the halls of their castle near the close of the play (V.i.30–34). Blood symbolizes the guilt that sits like a permanent stain on the consciences of both Macbeth and Lady Macbeth, one that hounds them to their graves.

THE WEATHER

As in other Shakespearean tragedies, Macbeth's grotesque murder spree is accompanied by a number of unnatural occurrences in the natural realm. From the thunder and lightning that accompany the witches' appearances to the terrible storms that rage on the night of Duncan's murder, these violations of the natural order reflect corruption in the moral and political orders.

SUMMARY & ANALYSIS

ACT I, SCENES I–IV

SUMMARY: ACT I, SCENE I
Thunder and lightning crash above a Scottish moor. Three haggard old women, the witches, appear out of the storm. In eerie, chanting tones, they make plans to meet again upon the heath, after the battle, to confront Macbeth. As quickly as they arrive, they disappear.

SUMMARY: ACT I, SCENE II
At a military camp near his palace at Forres, King Duncan of Scotland asks a wounded captain for news about the Scots' battle with the Irish invaders, who are led by the rebel Macdonald. The captain, who was wounded helping Duncan's son Malcolm escape capture by the Irish, replies that the Scottish generals Macbeth and Banquo fought with great courage and violence. The captain then describes for Duncan how Macbeth slew the traitorous Macdonald. As the captain is carried off to have his wounds attended to, the thane of Ross, a Scottish nobleman, enters and tells the king that the traitorous thane of Cawdor has been defeated and the army of Norway repelled. Duncan decrees that the thane of Cawdor be put to death and that Macbeth, the hero of the victorious army, be given Cawdor's title. Ross leaves to deliver the news to Macbeth.

SUMMARY: ACT I, SCENE III
On the heath near the battlefield, thunder rolls and the three witches appear. One says that she has just come from "[k]illing swine" and another describes the revenge she has planned upon a sailor whose wife refused to share her chestnuts. Suddenly a drum beats, and the third witch cries that Macbeth is coming. Macbeth and Banquo, on their way to the king's court at Forres, come upon the witches and shrink in horror at the sight of the old women. Banquo asks whether they are mortal, noting that they don't seem to be "inhabitants o' th' earth" (I.iii.39). He also wonders whether they are really women, since they seem to have beards like men. The witches hail Macbeth as thane of Glamis (his original title) and as thane of Cawdor. Macbeth is baffled by this second title, as he has not yet heard of King Duncan's decision. The witches also declare that Macbeth will be king one day. Stunned and intrigued, Macbeth presses the

17

witches for more information, but they have turned their attention to Banquo, speaking in yet more riddles. They call Banquo "lesser than Macbeth, and greater," and "not so happy, yet much happier"; then they tell him that he will never be king but that his children will sit upon the throne (I.iii.63–65). Macbeth implores the witches to explain what they meant by calling him thane of Cawdor, but they vanish into thin air.

In disbelief, Macbeth and Banquo discuss the strange encounter. Macbeth fixates on the details of the prophecy. "Your children shall be kings," he says to his friend, to which Banquo responds: "You shall be king" (I.iii.84). Their conversation is interrupted by the arrival of Ross and Angus, who have come to convey them to the king. Ross tells Macbeth that the king has made him thane of Cawdor, as the former thane is to be executed for treason. Macbeth, amazed that the witches' prophecy has come true, asks Banquo if he hopes his children will be kings. Banquo replies that devils often tell half-truths in order to "win us to our harm" (I.iii.121). Macbeth ignores his companions and speaks to himself, ruminating upon the possibility that he might one day be king. He wonders whether the reign will simply fall to him or whether he will have to perform a dark deed in order to gain the crown. At last he shakes himself from his reverie and the group departs for Forres. As they leave, Macbeth whispers to Banquo that, at a later time, he would like to speak to him privately about what has transpired.

SUMMARY: ACT I, SCENE IV

At the king's palace, Duncan hears reports of Cawdor's execution from his son Malcolm, who says that Cawdor died nobly, confessing freely and repenting of his crimes. Macbeth and Banquo enter with Ross and Angus. Duncan thanks the two generals profusely for their heroism in the battle, and they profess their loyalty and gratitude toward Duncan. Duncan announces his intention to name Malcolm the heir to his throne. Macbeth declares his joy but notes to himself that Malcolm now stands between him and the crown. Plans are made for Duncan to dine at Macbeth's castle that evening, and Macbeth goes on ahead of the royal party to inform his wife of the king's impending arrival.

ANALYSIS: ACT I, SCENES I–IV

These scenes establish the play's dramatic premise—the witches' awakening of Macbeth's ambition—and present the main characters and their relationships. At the same time, the first three scenes establish a dark mood that permeates the entire play. The stage directions indicate that the play begins with a storm, and malignant supernatural forces immediately appear in the form of the three witches. From there, the action quickly shifts to a battlefield that is dominated by a sense of the grisliness and cruelty of war. In his description of Macbeth and Banquo's heroics, the captain dwells specifically on images of carnage: "he unseamed him from the nave to th' chops," he says, describing Macbeth's slaying of Macdonald (I.ii.22). The bloody murders that fill the play are foreshadowed by the bloody victory that the Scots win over their enemies.

Our initial impression of Macbeth, based on the captain's report of his valor and prowess in battle, is immediately complicated by Macbeth's obvious fixation upon the witches' prophecy. Macbeth is a noble and courageous warrior but his reaction to the witches' pronouncements emphasizes his great desire for power and prestige. Macbeth immediately realizes that the fulfillment of the prophecy may require conspiracy and murder on his part. He clearly allows himself to consider taking such actions, although he is by no means resolved to do so. His reaction to the prophecy displays a fundamental confusion and inactivity: instead of resolving to act on the witches' claims, or simply dismissing them, Macbeth talks himself into a kind of thoughtful stupor as he tries to work out the situation for himself. In the following scene, Lady Macbeth will emerge and drive the hesitant Macbeth to act; she is the will propelling his achievements. Once Lady Macbeth hears of the witches' prophecy, Duncan's life is doomed.

Macbeth contains some of Shakespeare's most vivid female characters. Lady Macbeth and the three witches are extremely wicked, but they are also stronger and more imposing than the men around them. The sinister witches cast the mood for the entire play. Their rhyming incantations stand out eerily amid the blank verse spoken by the other characters, and their grotesque figures of speech establish a lingering aura. Whenever they appear, the stage directions deliberately link them to unease and lurking chaos in the natural world by insisting on "Thunder" or "Thunder and lightning."

Shakespeare has the witches speak in language of contradiction. Their famous line "Fair is foul, and foul is fair" is a prominent example (I.i.10), but there are many others, such as their characterization of Banquo as "lesser than Macbeth, and greater" (I.iii.63). Such speech adds to the play's sense of moral confusion by implying that nothing is quite what it seems. Interestingly, Macbeth's first line in the play is "So foul and fair a day I have not seen" (I.iii.36). This line echoes the witches' words and establishes a connection between them and Macbeth. It also suggests that Macbeth is the focus of the drama's moral confusion.

ACT I, SCENES V–VII

SUMMARY: ACT I, SCENE V

> ... Come, you spirits
> That tend on mortal thoughts, unsex me here,
> And fill me from the crown to the toe top-full
> Of direst cruelty.
>
> (See QUOTATIONS, p. 43)

In Inverness, Macbeth's castle, Lady Macbeth reads to herself a letter she has received from Macbeth. The letter announces Macbeth's promotion to the thaneship of Cawdor and details his meeting with the witches. Lady Macbeth murmurs that she knows Macbeth is ambitious, but fears he is too full of "th' milk of human kindness" to take the steps necessary to make himself king (I.v.15). She resolves to convince her husband to do whatever is required to seize the crown. A messenger enters and informs Lady Macbeth that the king rides toward the castle, and that Macbeth is on his way as well. As she awaits her husband's arrival, she delivers a famous speech in which she begs, "you spirits / That tend on mortal thoughts, unsex me here, / And fill me from the crown to the toe top-full / Of direst cruelty" (I.v.38–41). She resolves to put her natural femininity aside so that she can do the bloody deeds necessary to seize the crown. Macbeth enters, and he and his wife discuss the king's forthcoming visit. Macbeth tells his wife that Duncan plans to depart the next day, but Lady Macbeth declares that the king will never see tomorrow. She tells her husband to have patience and to leave the plan to her.

SUMMARY: ACT I, SCENE VI

Duncan, the Scottish lords, and their attendants arrive outside Macbeth's castle. Duncan praises the castle's pleasant environment, and he thanks Lady Macbeth, who has emerged to greet him, for her hospitality. She replies that it is her duty to be hospitable since she and her husband owe so much to their king. Duncan then asks to be taken inside to Macbeth, whom he professes to love dearly.

SUMMARY: ACT I, SCENE VII

> *If it were done when 'tis done, then 'twere well*
> *It were done quickly . . .*
> . . .
> *. . . He's here in double trust:*
> *First, as I am his kinsman and his subject,*
> *Strong both against the deed; then, as his host,*
> *Who should against his murderer shut the door,*
> *Not bear the knife myself.*
>
> *(See* QUOTATIONS, *p. 44)*

Inside the castle, as oboes play and servants set a table for the evening's feast, Macbeth paces by himself, pondering his idea of assassinating Duncan. He says that the deed would be easy if he could be certain that it would not set in motion a series of terrible consequences. He declares his willingness to risk eternal damnation but realizes that even on earth, bloody actions "return / To plague th'inventor" (I.vii.9–10). He then considers the reasons why he ought not to kill Duncan: Macbeth is Duncan's kinsman, subject, and host; moreover, the king is universally admired as a virtuous ruler. Macbeth notes that these circumstances offer him nothing that he can use to motivate himself. He faces the fact that there is no reason to kill the king other than his own ambition, which he realizes is an unreliable guide.

Lady Macbeth enters and tells her husband that the king has dined and that he has been asking for Macbeth. Macbeth declares that he no longer intends to kill Duncan. Lady Macbeth, outraged, calls him a coward and questions his manhood: "When you durst do it," she says, "then you were a man" (I.vii.49). He asks her what will happen if they fail; she promises that as long as they are bold, they will be successful. Then she tells him her plan: while Duncan sleeps, she will give his chamberlains wine to make them drunk, and then she and Macbeth can slip in and murder Duncan. They will smear the blood of Duncan on the sleeping chamberlains to cast the guilt upon them. Astonished at the brilliance and daring of her plan, Macbeth tells his wife that her "undaunted mettle" makes him hope that she will only give birth to male children (I.vii.73). He then agrees to proceed with the murder.

ANALYSIS: ACT I, SCENES V–VII

These scenes are dominated by Lady Macbeth, who is probably the most memorable character in the play. Her violent, blistering soliloquies in Act I, scenes v and vii, testify to her strength of will, which completely eclipses that of her husband. She is well aware of the discrepancy between their respective resolves and understands that she will have to manipulate her husband into acting on the witches' prophecy. Her soliloquy in Act I, scene v, begins the play's exploration of gender roles, particularly of the value and nature of masculinity. In the soliloquy, she spurns her feminine characteristics, crying out "unsex me here" and wishing that the milk in her breasts would be exchanged for "gall" so that she could murder Duncan herself. These remarks manifest Lady Macbeth's belief that manhood is defined by murder. When, in Act I, scene vii, her husband is hesitant to murder Duncan, she goads him by questioning his manhood and by implicitly comparing his willingness to carry through on his intention of killing Duncan with his ability to carry out a sexual act (I.vii.38–41). Throughout the play, whenever Macbeth shows signs of faltering, Lady Macbeth implies that he is less than a man.

Macbeth exclaims that Lady Macbeth should "[b]ring forth men-children only" because she is so bold and courageous (I.vii.72). Since Macbeth succumbs to Lady Macbeth's wishes immediately following this remark, it seems that he is complimenting her and affirming her belief that courage and brilliance are masculine traits. But the comment also suggests that Macbeth is thinking about his legacy. He sees Lady Macbeth's boldness and masculinity as heroic and warriorlike, while Lady Macbeth invokes her supposed masculine "virtues" for dark, cruel purposes. Unlike Macbeth, she seems solely concerned with immediate power.

A subject's loyalty to his king is one of the thematic concerns of *Macbeth*. The plot of the play hinges on Macbeth's betrayal of Duncan, and, ultimately, of Scotland. Just as Lady Macbeth will prove to be the antithesis of the ideal wife, Macbeth proves to be a completely disloyal subject. In Act I, scene vii, for instance, Macbeth muses on Duncan's many good qualities, reflects that Duncan has been kind to him, and thinks that perhaps he ought not to kill his king. This is Macbeth's first lengthy soliloquy and thus the audience's first peek inside his mind. Yet Macbeth is unable to quell his desire for power. He evades answering his own questions of loyalty and yearns unrealistically for the battlefield's simple and consequence-free action—"If it were done when 'tis done," he says, "then 'twere well / It were done quickly" (I.vii.1–2).

At the same time, Macbeth is strongly conscious of the gravity of the act of regicide. He acknowledges that "bloody instructions . . . being taught, return / To plague th'inventor" (I.vii.9–10). This is the first of many lines linking "blood" to guilt and cosmic retribution.

As her husband wavers, Lady Macbeth enters like a hurricane and blows his hesitant thoughts away. She spurs Macbeth to treason by disregarding his rational, moral arguments and challenging his manhood. Basically, she dares him to commit the murder, using words that taunt rather than persuade. Under her spell, all of Macbeth's objections seem to evaporate and he is left only with a weak "If we should fail?" to set against her passionate challenge (I.vii.59).

The idea of a moral order is present in these scenes, albeit in muted form. Macbeth knows what he does is wrong, and he recognizes that there will surely be consequences. As we have seen, his soliloquy reveals his awareness that he may be initiating a cycle of violence that will eventually destroy him. Macbeth is not a *good* man at this point in the play, but he is not yet an evil one—he is tempted, and he tries to resist temptation. Macbeth's resistance, however, is not vigorous enough to stand up to his wife's ability to manipulate him.

ACT II, SCENES I–II

SUMMARY: ACT II, SCENE I
Banquo and his son Fleance walk in the torch-lit hall of Macbeth's castle. Fleance says that it is after midnight, and his father responds that although he is tired, he wishes to stay awake because his sleep has lately inspired "cursed thoughts" (II.i.8). Macbeth enters, and Banquo is surprised to see him still up. Banquo says that the king is asleep and mentions that he had a dream about the "three weird sisters." When Banquo suggests that the witches have revealed "some truth" to Macbeth, Macbeth claims that he has not thought of them at all since their encounter in the woods (II.i.19–20). He and Banquo agree to discuss the witches' prophecies at a later time.

Banquo and Fleance leave, and suddenly, in the darkened hall, Macbeth has a vision of a dagger floating in the air before him, its handle pointing toward his hand and its tip aiming him toward Duncan. Macbeth tries to grasp the weapon and fails. He wonders whether what he sees is real or a "dagger of the mind, a false creation / Proceeding from the heat-oppressed brain" (II.i.38–39). Continuing to gaze upon the dagger, he thinks he sees blood on the blade, then abruptly decides that the vision is just a manifestation of his unease over killing Duncan. The night around him seems thick with horror and witchcraft, but Macbeth stiffens and resolves to do his bloody work. A bell tolls—Lady Macbeth's signal that the chamberlains are asleep—and Macbeth strides toward Duncan's chamber.

SUMMARY: ACT II, SCENE II

> *Will all great Neptune's ocean wash this blood*
> *Clean from my hand? No, this my hand will rather*
> *The multitudinous seas incarnadine,*
> *Making the green one red.*
>
> (See QUOTATIONS, *p. 45*)

As Macbeth leaves the hall, Lady Macbeth enters, remarking on her boldness. She imagines that Macbeth is killing the king even as she speaks. Hearing Macbeth cry out, she worries that the chamberlains have awakened. She says that she cannot understand how Macbeth could fail—she had prepared the daggers for the chamberlains herself. She asserts that she would have killed the king herself then and there, "[h]ad he not resembled / [her] father as he slept" (II.ii.12–13). Macbeth emerges, his hands covered in blood, and says that the deed is done. Badly shaken, he remarks that he heard the chamberlains awake and say their prayers before going back to sleep. When they said "amen," he tried to say it with them but found that the word stuck in his throat. He adds that as he killed the king, he thought he heard a voice cry out: "Sleep no more, / Macbeth does murder sleep" (II.ii.33–34).

Lady Macbeth at first tries to steady her husband, but she becomes angry when she notices that he has forgotten to leave the daggers with the sleeping chamberlains so as to frame them for Duncan's murder. He refuses to go back into the room, so she takes the daggers into the room herself, saying that she would be ashamed to be as cowardly as Macbeth. As she leaves, Macbeth hears a mysterious knocking. The portentous sound frightens him, and he asks desperately, "Will all great Neptune's ocean wash this blood / Clean from my hand?" (II.ii.58–59). As Lady Macbeth reenters the hall, the knocking comes again, and then a third time. She leads her husband back to the bedchamber, where he can wash off the blood.

"A little water clears us of this deed," she tells him. "How easy it is then!" (II.ii.65–66).

ANALYSIS: ACT II, SCENES I–II

Banquo's knowledge of the witches' prophecy makes him both a potential ally and a potential threat to Macbeth's plotting. For now, Macbeth seems distrustful of Banquo and pretends to have hardly thought of the witches, but Macbeth's desire to discuss the prophecies at some future time suggests that he may have some sort of conspiratorial plans in mind. The appearance of Fleance, Banquo's son, serves as a reminder of the witches' prediction that Banquo's children will sit on the throne of Scotland. We realize that if Macbeth succeeds in the murder of Duncan, he will be driven to still more violence before his crown is secure, and Fleance will be in immediate and mortal danger.

Act II is singularly concerned with the murder of Duncan. But Shakespeare here relies on a technique that he uses throughout *Macbeth* to help sustain the play's incredibly rapid tempo of development: elision. We see the scenes leading up to the murder and the scenes immediately following it, but the deed itself does not appear onstage. Duncan's bedchamber becomes a sort of hidden sanctum into which the characters disappear and from which they emerge powerfully changed. This technique of not allowing us to see the actual murder, which persists throughout *Macbeth*, may have been borrowed from the classical Greek tragedies of Aeschylus and Sophocles. In these plays, violent acts abound but are kept offstage, made to seem more terrible by the power of suggestion. The effect on Lady Macbeth of her trip into Duncan's bedroom is particularly striking. She claims that she would have killed Duncan herself except that he resembled her father sleeping. This is the first time Lady Macbeth shows herself to be at all vulnerable. Her comparison of Duncan to her father suggests that despite her desire for power and her harsh chastisement of Macbeth, she sees her king as an authority figure to whom she must be loyal.

Macbeth's trepidation about the murder is echoed by several portentous sounds and visions, the famous hallucinatory dagger being the most striking. The dagger is the first in a series of guilt-inspired hallucinations that Macbeth and his wife experience. The murder is also marked by the ringing of the bell and the knocking at the gate, both of which have fascinated audiences. The knocking occurs four times with a sort of ritualistic regularity. It conveys the heavy sense of the inevitable, as if the gates must eventually open to admit doom. The knocking seems particularly ironic after we realize that Macduff, who kills Macbeth at the end of the play, is its source. Macbeth's eventual death does indeed stand embodied at the gate.

The motif of blood, established in the accounts of Macbeth's and Banquo's battlefield exploits, recurs here in Macbeth's anguished sense that there is blood on his hands that cannot be washed clean. For now, Lady Macbeth remains the voice of calculating reason, as she tells him that the blood can be washed away with a little water. But, as Lady Macbeth eventually realizes, the guilt that the blood symbolizes needs more than water to be cleansed away. Her hallucinations later in the play, in which she washes her hands obsessively, lend irony to her insistence here that "[a] little water clears us of this deed" (II.ii.65).

ACT II, SCENES III–IV

SUMMARY: ACT II, SCENE III

A porter stumbles through the hallway to answer the knocking, grumbling comically about the noise and mocking whoever is on the other side of the door. He compares himself to a porter at the gates of hell and asks, "Who's there, i' th' name of Beelzebub?" (II.iii.3). Macduff and Lennox enter, and Macduff complains about the porter's slow response to his knock. The porter says that he was up late carousing and rambles on humorously about the effects of alcohol, which he says provokes red noses, sleepiness, and urination. He adds that drink also "provokes and unprovokes" lechery—it inclines one to be lustful but takes away the ability to have sex (II.iii.27). Macbeth enters, and Macduff asks him if the king is awake, saying that Duncan asked to see him early that morning. In short, clipped sentences, Macbeth says that Duncan is still asleep. He offers to take Macduff to the king. As Macduff enters the king's chamber, Lennox describes the storms that raged the previous night, asserting that he cannot remember anything like it in all his years. With a cry of "O horror, horror, horror!" Macduff comes running from the room, shouting that the king has been murdered (II.iii.59). Macbeth and Lennox rush in to look, while Lady Macbeth appears and expresses her horror that such a deed could be done under her roof. General chaos ensues as the other nobles and their servants come streaming in. As Macbeth and Lennox emerge from the bedroom, Malcolm and Donalbain arrive on the scene. They are told that their father has been killed, most likely by his chamberlains, who were found with bloody daggers. Macbeth declares that in his rage he has killed the chamberlains.

Macduff seems suspicious of these new deaths, which Macbeth explains by saying that his fury at Duncan's death was so powerful that he could not restrain himself. Lady Macbeth suddenly faints, and both Macduff and Banquo call for someone to attend to her. Malcolm and Donalbain whisper to each other that they are not safe, since whoever killed their father will probably try to kill them next. Lady Macbeth is taken away, while Banquo and Macbeth rally the lords to meet and discuss the murder. Duncan's sons resolve to flee the court. Malcolm declares that he will go south to England, and Donalbain will hasten to Ireland.

SUMMARY: ACT II, SCENE IV

Ross, a thane, walks outside the castle with an old man. They discuss the strange and ominous happenings of the past few days: it is daytime, but dark outside; last Tuesday, an owl killed a falcon; and Duncan's beautiful, well-trained horses behaved wildly and ate one another. Macduff emerges from the castle and tells Ross that Macbeth has been made king by the other lords, and that he now rides to Scone to be crowned. Macduff adds that the chamberlains seem the most likely murderers, and that they may have been paid off by someone to kill Duncan. Suspicion has now fallen on the two princes, Malcolm and Donalbain, because they have fled the scene. Macduff returns to his home at Fife, and Ross departs for Scone to see the new king's coronation.

ANALYSIS: ACT II, SCENES III–IV

After the bloody imagery and dark tone of the previous two scenes, the porter's comedy comes as a jarring change of tone. His good-natured joking with Macduff breaks up the mounting tension of the play and also comments obliquely on its themes. Unlike all the characters of noble birth, who speak in iambic verse, the porter speaks in prose. His relaxed language seems to signal that his words and his role are less important than those of the other characters, but in his merry banter the porter hits on many truths. His description of the confusion and lust provoked by alcohol caricatures Macbeth's moral confusion and lust for power. Moreover, his remarks about the ineffective lechery inspired by drink eerily echo Lady Macbeth's sexual taunting of Macbeth about his ability to carry out his resolutions. The porter's joke that the door of Inverness is like hell's gate is ironic, given the cruel and bloody events that are taking place within the castle. When he cries, "Who's there, i' th' name of Beelzebub [the devil]?" the analogy between hell and Inverness becomes even stronger (II.iii.3). Instead of receiving a welcome and a blessing when they step into Macbeth's castle, guests are warned that they are putting themselves in the hands of the devil.

Now that Lady Macbeth's machinations have wrought their result, Lady Macbeth begins to recede from center stage and Macbeth takes her place as the most compelling character in the play. The clipped, halting sentences with which Macbeth speaks to Macduff and Lennox indicate his troubled mind and trepidation about the impending discovery of Duncan's body. For example, while Lennox offers a lengthy speech about the wild weather of the previous night, Macbeth's only response is a terse "'Twas a rough night" (II.iii.57). And when Lennox asks Macbeth, "Goes the King hence today?" Macbeth almost gives away his knowledge that Duncan is dead (II.iii.49). "He does," answers Macbeth, before he realizes that his answer is incriminating and changes it to: "[H]e did appoint so" (II.iii.49).

Once Duncan's body is discovered, it is as though a switch has been flipped within Macbeth. He springs into action with a clear eye toward his purpose, seizing control of the nobles and becoming King of Scotland. Interestingly, Shakespeare does not show us the scene in which Macbeth is made king. Just as he denied us the scene of Duncan's murder, he now skips over its most direct consequence, Macbeth's election. The news is conveyed secondhand through the characters of Ross, Macduff, and the old man.

Although Macbeth seems to gain confidence as Act II, scene iii, progresses, other characters subtly cast suspicion on him. When Malcolm asks about his father's killer, Lennox replies, "Those of his chamber, as it seemed, had done't" (II.iii.98). Lennox's insertion of "as it seemed" highlights the suspect nature of the crime scene's appearance. Banquo, also, expresses his wariness of Macbeth's argument that the chamberlains were the murderers. He says: "let us meet / And question this most bloody piece of work, / To know it further" (II.iii.123–125). By far, though, the most distrusting character is Macduff, who, up until this point in the play, has been a fairly unobtrusive character. He asks Macbeth why he killed the chamberlains, and later expresses his suspicion to Ross and the old man. His decision to return home to Fife rather than travel to Scone to see Macbeth's coronation is an open display of opposition. Thus, in a few swift strokes, the play establishes Macduff as Macbeth's eventual nemesis. Malcolm, of course, is the rightful king, but he lacks Macduff's initiative and sense of purpose, a fact illustrated by his willingness to flee rather than assert his royal rights. In order to regain the throne, he will need the aid of the more assertive Macduff—and it is Macduff, not Malcolm, who assumes the responsibility for Macbeth's death.

The conversation between Ross and the old man at the beginning of Act II, scene iv, tells the audience about a number of unnatural occurrences in the weather and the behavior of animals, which cast a menacing shadow over Macbeth's ascension to the throne. In Shakespeare's tragedies (*Julius Caesar, King Lear,* and *Hamlet,* in particular), terrible supernatural occurrences often betoken wicked behavior on the part of the characters and tragic consequences for the state. The storms that accompany the witches' appearances and Duncan's murder are more than mere atmospheric disturbances; they are symbols of the connection between moral, natural, and political developments in the universe of Shakespeare's plays. By killing Duncan, Macbeth unleashes a kind of primal chaos upon the realm of Scotland, in which the old order of benevolent king and loyal subjects is replaced by a darker relationship between a tyrant and his victims.

ACT III, SCENES I–III

SUMMARY: ACT III, SCENE I

In the royal palace at Forres, Banquo paces and thinks about the coronation of Macbeth and the prophecies of the weird sisters. The witches foretold that Macbeth would be king and that Banquo's line would eventually sit on the throne. If the first prophecy came true, Banquo thinks, feeling the stirring of ambition, why not the second? Macbeth enters, attired as king. He is followed by Lady Macbeth, now his queen, and the court. Macbeth and Lady Macbeth ask Banquo to attend the feast they will host that night. Banquo accepts their invitation and says that he plans to go for a ride on his horse for the afternoon. Macbeth mentions that they should discuss the problem of Malcolm and Donalbain. The brothers have fled from Scotland and may be plotting against his crown.

Banquo departs, and Macbeth dismisses his court. He is left alone in the hall with a single servant, to whom he speaks about some men who have come to see him. Macbeth asks if the men are still waiting and orders that they be fetched. Once the servant has gone, Macbeth begins a soliloquy. He muses on the subject of Banquo, reflecting that his old friend is the only man in Scotland whom he fears. He notes that if the witches' prophecy is true, his will be a "fruitless crown," by which he means that he will not have an heir (III.i.62). The murder of Duncan, which weighs so heavily on his conscience, may have simply cleared the way for Banquo's sons to overthrow Macbeth's own family.

The servant reenters with Macbeth's two visitors. Macbeth reminds the two men, who are murderers he has hired, of a conversation he had with them the day before, in which he chronicled the wrongs Banquo had done them in the past. He asks if they are angry and manly enough to take revenge on Banquo. They reply that they are, and Macbeth accepts their promise that they will murder his former friend. Macbeth reminds the murderers that Fleance must be killed along with his father and tells them to wait within the castle for his command.

SUMMARY: ACT III, SCENE II

Elsewhere in the castle, Lady Macbeth expresses despair and sends a servant to fetch her husband. Macbeth enters and tells his wife that he too is discontented, saying that his mind is "full of scorpions" (III.ii.37). He feels that the business that they began by killing Duncan is not yet complete because there are still threats to the throne that must be eliminated. Macbeth tells his wife that he has planned "a deed of dreadful note" for Banquo and Fleance and urges her to be jovial and kind to Banquo during the evening's feast, in order to lure their next victim into a false sense of security (III.ii.45).

SUMMARY: ACT III, SCENE III

It is dusk, and the two murderers, now joined by a third, linger in a wooded park outside the palace. Banquo and Fleance approach on their horses and dismount. They light a torch, and the murderers set upon them. The murderers kill Banquo, who dies urging his son to flee and to avenge his death. One of the murderers extinguishes the torch, and in the darkness Fleance escapes. The murderers leave with Banquo's body to find Macbeth and tell him what has happened.

ANALYSIS: ACT III, SCENES I–III

After his first confrontation with the witches, Macbeth worried that he would have to commit a murder to gain the Scottish crown. He seems to have gotten used to the idea, as by this point the body count has risen to alarming levels. Now that the first part of the witches' prophecy has come true, Macbeth feels that he must kill his friend Banquo and the young Fleance in order to prevent the second part from becoming realized. But, as Fleance's survival suggests, there can be no escape from the witches' prophecies.

Macbeth and his wife seem to have traded roles. As he talks to the murderers, Macbeth adopts the same rhetoric that Lady Macbeth used to convince him to murder in Act I, scene vii. He questions their manhood in order to make them angry, and their desire to murder Banquo and Fleance grows out of their desire to prove themselves to be men. In the scene with Lady Macbeth that follows, Macbeth again echoes her previous comments. She told him earlier that he must "look like the innocent flower, / But be the serpent under't" (I.v.63–64). Now he is the one reminding her to mask her unease, as he says that they must "make [their] faces visors to [their] hearts, / Disguising what they are" (III.ii.35–36). Yet, despite his displays of fearlessness, Macbeth is undeniably beset with guilt and doubt, which he expresses in his reference to the "scorpions" in his mind and in his declaration that in killing Banquo they "have scorched the snake, not killed it" (III.ii.15).

While her husband grows bolder, Lady Macbeth begins to despair—"Naught's had; all's spent," she says (III.ii.6). It is difficult to believe that the woman who now attempts to talk her husband out of committing more murders is the same Lady Macbeth who earlier spurred her husband on to slaughter. Just as he begins to echo her earlier statements, she references his. "What's done is done" (III.ii.14), she says wishfully, echoing her husband's use of "done" in Act I, scene vii, where he said: "If it were done when 'tis done, then 'twere well / It were done quickly" (I.vii.1–2). But as husband and wife begin to realize, nothing is "done" whatsoever; their sense of closure is an illusion.

Both characters seem shocked and dismayed that possessing the crown has not rid them of trouble or brought them happiness. The language that they use is fraught with imagery suggestive of suspicion, paranoia, and inner turmoil, like Macbeth's evocative "full of scorpions is my mind, dear wife" (III.ii.37). Each murder Macbeth commits or commissions is intended to bring him security and contentment, but the deeper his arms sink in blood, the more violent and horrified he becomes.

By the start of Act III, the play's main theme—the repercussions of acting on ambition without moral constraint—has been articulated and explored. The play now builds inexorably toward its end. Unlike *Hamlet,* in which the plot seems open to multiple possibilities up to the final scene, *Macbeth*'s action seems to develop inevitably. We know that there is nothing to stop Macbeth's murder spree except his own death, and it is for that death that the audience now waits. Only with Macbeth's demise, we realize, can any kind of moral order be restored to Scotland.

ACT III, SCENES IV–VI

SUMMARY: ACT III, SCENE IV

Onstage stands a table heaped with a feast. Macbeth and Lady Macbeth enter as king and queen, followed by their court, whom they bid welcome. As Macbeth walks among the company, the first murderer appears at the doorway. Macbeth speaks to him for a moment, learning that Banquo is dead and that Fleance has escaped. The news of Fleance's escape angers Macbeth—if only Fleance had died, he muses, his throne would have been secure. Instead, "the worm that's fled / Hath nature that in time will venom breed" (III.iv.28–29).

Returning to his guests, Macbeth goes to sit at the head of the royal table but finds Banquo's ghost sitting in his chair. Horror-struck, Macbeth speaks to the ghost, which is invisible to the rest of the company. Lady Macbeth makes excuses for her husband, saying that he occasionally has such "visions" and that the guests should simply ignore his behavior. Then she speaks to Macbeth, questioning his manhood and urging him to snap out of his trance. The ghost disappears, and Macbeth recovers, telling his company: "I have a strange infirmity which is nothing / To those that know me" (III.iv.85–86). As he offers a toast to company, however, Banquo's specter reappears and shocks Macbeth into further reckless outbursts. Continuing to make excuses for her husband, Lady Macbeth sends the alarmed guests out of the room as the ghost vanishes again.

Macbeth mutters that "blood will have blood" and tells Lady Macbeth that he has heard from a servant-spy that Macduff intends to keep away from court, behavior that verges on treason (III.iv.121). He says that he will visit the witches again tomorrow in the hopes of learning more about the future and about who may be plotting against him. He resolves to do whatever is necessary to keep his throne, declaring: "I am in blood / Stepped in so far that, should I wade no more, / Returning were as tedious as go o'er" (III.iv.135–137). Lady Macbeth says that he needs sleep, and they retire to their bed.

Summary: Act III, scene v

Upon the stormy heath, the witches meet with Hecate, the goddess of witchcraft. Hecate scolds them for meddling in the business of Macbeth without consulting her but declares that she will take over as supervisor of the mischief. She says that when Macbeth comes the next day, as they know he will, they must summon visions and spirits whose messages will fill him with a false sense of security and "draw him on to his confusion" (III.v.29). Hecate vanishes, and the witches go to prepare their charms.

Summary: Act III, scene vi

That night, somewhere in Scotland, Lennox walks with another lord, discussing what has happened to the kingdom. Banquo's murder has been officially blamed on Fleance, who has fled. Nevertheless, both men suspect Macbeth, whom they call a "tyrant," in the murders of Duncan and Banquo. The lord tells Lennox that Macduff has gone to England, where he will join Malcolm in pleading with England's King Edward for aid. News of these plots has prompted Macbeth to prepare for war. Lennox and the lord express their hope that Malcolm and Macduff will be successful and that their actions can save Scotland from Macbeth.

Analysis: Act III, scenes iv–vi

Throughout *Macbeth,* as in many of Shakespeare's tragedies, the supernatural and the unnatural appear in grotesque form as harbingers of wickedness, moral corruption, and downfall. Here, the appearance of Banquo's silent ghost, the reappearance of the witches, and the introduction of the goddess Hecate all symbolize the corruption of Scotland's political and moral health. In place of the dramatization of Macbeth's acts of despotism, Shakespeare uses the scenes involving supernatural elements to increase the audience's sense of foreboding and ill omen. When Macbeth's political transgressions are revealed, Scotland's dire situation immediately registers, because the transgressions of state have been predicted by the disturbances in nature. In Macbeth's moral landscape, loyalty, honor, and virtue serve either as weak or nonexistent constraints against ambition and the lust for power. In the physical landscape that surrounds him, the normal rules of nature serve as weak constraints against the grotesqueries of the witches and the horrific ghost of Banquo.

The banquet is simultaneously the high point of Macbeth's reign and the beginning of his downfall. Macbeth's bizarre behavior puzzles and disturbs his subjects, confirming their impression that he is mentally troubled. Despite the tentativeness and guilt she displayed in the previous scene, Lady Macbeth here appears surefooted and stronger than her husband, but even her attempts to explain away her husband's "hallucination" are ineffective when paired with the evidence of his behavior. The contrast between this scene and the one in which Duncan's body was discovered is striking—whereas Macbeth was once cold-blooded and surefooted, he now allows his anxieties and visions to get the best of him.

It is unclear whether Banquo's ghost really sits in Macbeth's chair or whether the spirit's presence is only a hallucination inspired by guilt. *Macbeth,* of course, is thick with supernatural events and characters, so there is no reason to discount the possibility that a ghost actually stalks the halls. Some of the apparitions that appear in the play, such as the floating dagger in Act II, scene i, and the unwashable blood that Lady Macbeth perceives on her hands in Act IV, appear to be more psychological than supernatural in origin, but even this is uncertain. These recurring apparitions or hallucinations reflect the sense of metaphysical dread that consumes the royal couple as they feel the fateful force of their deeds coming back to haunt them.

Given the role that Banquo's character plays in *Macbeth,* it is appropriate that he and not Duncan should haunt Macbeth. Like Macbeth, Banquo heard the witches' prophecies and entertained ambitions. But, unlike Macbeth, Banquo took no criminal action. His actions stand as a rebuke to Macbeth's behavior and represent a path not taken, one in which ambition need not beget bloodshed. In *Holinshed's Chronicles,* the history that served as the source for Shakespeare's *Macbeth,* Banquo was Macbeth's accomplice in Duncan's murder. Shakespeare most likely changed Banquo's role from villain to moral pillar because Shakespeare's patron, King James I of England, was believed to be Banquo's descendant.

Shakespeare also portrays the historical figure of King Edward the Confessor, to whom Malcolm and Macduff have gone to receive help combating Macbeth. Edward is presented as the complete opposite of the evil, corrupt Macbeth. By including mention of England and Scotland's cooperation in the play, Shakespeare emphasizes that the bond between the two countries, renewed in his time by James's kingship, is a long-standing one. At the same time, the fact that Macbeth's opposition coalesces in England is at once a suggestion that Scotland has become too thoroughly corrupted to resist Macbeth and a self-congratulatory nod to Shakespeare's English audience.

ACT IV, SCENES I–III

SUMMARY: ACT IV, SCENE I

In a dark cavern, a bubbling cauldron hisses and spits, and the three witches suddenly appear onstage. They circle the cauldron, chanting spells and adding bizarre ingredients to their stew—"eye of newt and toe of frog, / Wool of bat and tongue of dog" (IV.i.14–15). Hecate materializes and compliments the witches on their work. One of the witches then chants: "By the pricking of my thumbs, / Something wicked this way comes" (IV.i.61–62). In fulfillment of the witch's prediction, Macbeth enters. He asks the witches to reveal the truth of their prophecies to him. To answer his questions, they summon horrible apparitions, each of which offers a prediction to allay Macbeth's fears. First, a floating head warns him to beware Macduff; Macbeth says that he has already guessed as much. Then a bloody child appears and tells him that "none of woman born / shall harm Macbeth" (IV.i.96–97). Next, a crowned child holding a tree tells him that he is safe until Birnam Wood moves to Dunsinane Hill. Finally, a procession of eight crowned kings walks by, the last carrying a mirror. Banquo's ghost walks at the end of the line. Macbeth demands to know the meaning of this final vision, but the witches perform a mad dance and then vanish. Lennox enters and tells Macbeth that Macduff has fled to England. Macbeth resolves to send murderers to capture Macduff's castle and to kill Macduff's wife and children.

SUMMARY: ACT IV, SCENE II

At Macduff's castle, Lady Macduff accosts Ross, demanding to know why her husband has fled. She feels betrayed. Ross insists that she trust her husband's judgment and then regretfully departs. Once he is gone, Lady Macduff tells her son that his father is dead, but the little boy perceptively argues that he is not. Suddenly, a messenger hurries in, warning Lady Macduff that she is in danger and urging her to flee. Lady Macduff protests, arguing that she has done no wrong. A group of murderers then enters. When one of them denounces Macduff, Macduff's son calls the murderer a liar, and the murderer stabs him. Lady Macduff turns and runs, and the pack of killers chases after her.

Summary: Act IV, scene iii

Outside King Edward's palace, Malcolm speaks with Macduff, telling him that he does not trust him since he has left his family in Scotland and may be secretly working for Macbeth. To determine whether Macduff is trustworthy, Malcolm rambles on about his own vices. He admits that he wonders whether he is fit to be king, since he claims to be lustful, greedy, and violent. At first, Macduff politely disagrees with his future king, but eventually Macduff cannot keep himself from crying out, "O Scotland, Scotland!" (IV.iii.101). Macduff's loyalty to Scotland leads him to agree that Malcolm is not fit to govern Scotland and perhaps not even to live. In giving voice to his disparagement, Macduff has passed Malcolm's test of loyalty. Malcolm then retracts the lies he has put forth about his supposed shortcomings and embraces Macduff as an ally. A doctor appears briefly and mentions that a "crew of wretched souls" waits for King Edward so they may be cured (IV.iii.142). When the doctor leaves, Malcolm explains to Macduff that King Edward has a miraculous power to cure disease.

Ross enters. He has just arrived from Scotland, and tells Macduff that his wife and children are well. He urges Malcolm to return to his country, listing the woes that have befallen Scotland since Macbeth took the crown. Malcolm says that he will return with ten thousand soldiers lent him by the English king. Then, breaking down, Ross confesses to Macduff that Macbeth has murdered his wife and children. Macduff is crushed with grief. Malcolm urges him to turn his grief to anger, and Macduff assures him that he will inflict revenge upon Macbeth.

Analysis: Act IV, scenes i–iii

The witches are vaguely absurd figures, with their rhymes and beards and capering, but they are also clearly sinister, possessing a great deal of power over events. Are they simply independent agents playing mischievously and cruelly with human events? Or are the "weird sisters" agents of fate, betokening the inevitable? The word *weird* descends etymologically from the Anglo-Saxon word *wyrd,* which means "fate" or "doom," and the three witches bear a striking resemblance to the Fates, female characters in both Norse and Greek mythology. Perhaps their prophecies are constructed to wreak havoc in the minds of the hearers, so that they become self-fulfilling. It is doubtful, for instance, that Macbeth would have killed Duncan if not for his meeting with the witches. On the other hand, the sisters' prophecies may be accurate readings of the future. After all, when Birnam Wood comes to Dunsinane at the play's end, the soldiers bearing the branches have not heard of the prophecy.

Whatever the nature of the witches' prophecies, their sheer inscrutability is as important as any reading of their motivations and natures. The witches stand outside the limits of human comprehension. They seem to represent the part of human beings in which ambition and sin originate—an incomprehensible and unconscious part of the human psyche. In this sense, they almost seem to belong to a Christian framework, as supernatural embodiments of the Christian concept of original sin. Indeed, many critics have argued that *Macbeth,* a remarkably simple story of temptation, fall, and retribution, is the most explicitly Christian of Shakespeare's great tragedies. If so, however, it is a dark Christianity, one more concerned with the bloody consequences of sin than with grace or divine love. Perhaps it would be better to say that *Macbeth* is the most orderly and just of the tragedies, insofar as evil deeds lead first to psychological torment and then to destruction. The nihilism of *King Lear,* in which the very idea of divine justice seems laughable, is absent in *Macbeth*—divine justice, whether Christian or not, is a palpable force hounding Macbeth toward his inevitable end.

The witches' prophecies allow Macbeth, whose sense of doom is mounting, to tell himself that everything may yet be well. For the audience, which lacks Macbeth's misguided confidence, the strange apparitions act as symbols that foreshadow the way the prophecies will be fulfilled. The armored head suggests war or rebellion, a telling image when connected to the apparition's warning about Macduff. The bloody child obliquely refers to Macduff's birth by cesarean section—he is not "of woman born"—attaching a clear irony to a comment that Macbeth takes at face value. The crowned child is Malcolm. He carries a tree, just as his soldiers will later carry tree branches from Birnam Wood to Dunsinane. Finally, the procession of kings reveals the future line of kings, all descended from Banquo. Some of those kings carry two balls and three scepters, the royal insignia of Great Britain—alluding to the fact that James I, Shakespeare's patron, claimed descent from the historical Banquo. The mirror carried by the last figure may have been meant to reflect King James, sitting in the audience, to himself.

The murder of Lady Macduff and her young son in Act IV, scene ii, marks the moment in which Macbeth descends into utter madness, killing neither for political gain nor to silence an enemy, but simply out of a furious desire to do harm. As Malcolm and Macduff reason in Act IV, scene iii, Macbeth's is the worst possible method of kingship. It is a political approach without moral legitimacy because it is not founded on loyalty to the state. Their conversation reflects an important theme in the play—the nature of true kingship, which is embodied by Duncan and King Edward, as opposed to the tyranny of Macbeth. In the end, a true king seems to be one motivated by love of his kingdom more than by pure self-interest. In a sense, both Malcolm and Macduff share this virtue—the love they hold for Scotland unites them in opposition to Macbeth, and grants their attempt to seize power a moral legitimacy that Macbeth's lacked.

Macduff and Malcolm are allies, but Macduff also serves as a teacher to Malcolm. Malcolm believes himself to be crafty and intuitive, as his test of Macduff shows. Yet, he has a perverted idea of manhood that is in line with Macbeth's. When Ross brings word of Lady Macduff's murder, Malcolm tells Macduff: "Dispute it like a man" (IV.iii.221). Macduff answers, "I shall do so, / But I must also feel it as a man" (IV.iii.222–223). Macduff shows that manhood comprises of more than aggression and murder; allowing oneself to be sensitive and to feel grief is also necessary. This is an important lesson for Malcolm to learn if he is to be a judicious, honest, and compassionate king. When, in Act V, scene xi, Malcolm voices his sorrow for Siward's son, he demonstrates that he has taken Macduff's instruction to heart.

ACT V, SCENES I–XI

SUMMARY: ACT V, SCENE I

> *Out, damned spot; out, I say.* . . . *Yet who would have thought the old man to have had so much blood in him?*
>
> *(See* QUOTATIONS, *p. 46)*

At night, in the king's palace at Dunsinane, a doctor and a gentlewoman discuss Lady Macbeth's strange habit of sleepwalking. Suddenly, Lady Macbeth enters in a trance with a candle in her hand. Bemoaning the murders of Lady Macduff and Banquo, she seems to see blood on her hands and claims that nothing will ever wash it off.

She leaves, and the doctor and gentlewoman marvel at her descent into madness.

SUMMARY: ACT V, SCENE II

Outside the castle, a group of Scottish lords discusses the military situation: the English army approaches, led by Malcolm, and the Scottish army will meet them near Birnam Wood, apparently to join forces with them. The "tyrant," as Lennox and the other lords call Macbeth, has fortified Dunsinane Castle and is making his military preparations in a mad rage.

SUMMARY: ACT V, SCENE III

Macbeth strides into the hall of Dunsinane with the doctor and his attendants, boasting proudly that he has nothing to fear from the English army or from Malcolm, since "none of woman born" can harm him (IV.i.96) and since he will rule securely "[t]ill Birnam Wood remove to Dunsinane" (V.iii.2). He calls his servant Seyton, who confirms that an army of ten thousand Englishmen approaches the castle. Macbeth insists upon wearing his armor, though the battle is still some time off. The doctor tells the king that Lady Macbeth is kept from rest by "thick-coming fancies," and Macbeth orders him to cure her of her delusions (V.iii.40).

SUMMARY: ACT V, SCENE IV

In the country near Birnam Wood, Malcolm talks with the English lord Siward and his officers about Macbeth's plan to defend the fortified castle. They decide that each soldier should cut down a bough of the forest and carry it in front of him as they march to the castle, thereby disguising their numbers.

SUMMARY: ACT V, SCENE V

> Life's but a walking shadow, a poor player
> That struts and frets his hour upon the stage,
> And then is heard no more. It is a tale
> Told by an idiot, full of sound and fury,
> Signifying nothing.

(See QUOTATIONS, *p. 47)*

Within the castle, Macbeth blusteringly orders that banners be hung and boasts that his castle will repel the enemy. A woman's cry is heard, and Seyton appears to tell Macbeth that the queen is dead. Shocked, Macbeth speaks numbly about the passage of time and declares famously that life is "a tale / Told by an idiot, full of sound and fury, / Signifying nothing" (V.v.25–27). A messenger enters with astonishing news: the trees of Birnam Wood are advancing toward Dunsinane. Enraged and terrified, Macbeth recalls the prophecy that said he could not die till Birnam Wood moved to Dunsinane. Resignedly, he declares that he is tired of the sun and that at least he will die fighting.

SUMMARY: ACT V, SCENE VI
Outside the castle, the battle commences. Malcolm orders the English soldiers to throw down their boughs and draw their swords.

SUMMARY: ACT V, SCENE VII
On the battlefield, Macbeth strikes those around him vigorously, insolent because no man born of woman can harm him. He slays Lord Siward's son and disappears in the fray.

SUMMARY: ACT V, SCENE VIII
Macduff emerges and searches the chaos frantically for Macbeth, whom he longs to cut down personally. He dives again into the battle.

SUMMARY: ACT V, SCENE IX
Malcolm and Siward emerge and enter the castle.

SUMMARY: ACT V, SCENE X
Elsewhere on the battlefield, Macbeth at last encounters Macduff. They fight, and when Macbeth insists that he is invincible because of the witches' prophecy, Macduff tells Macbeth that he was not of woman born, but rather "from his mother's womb / Untimely ripped" (V.x.15–16). Macbeth suddenly fears for his life, but he declares that he will not surrender "[t]o kiss the ground before young Malcolm's feet, / And to be baited with the rabble's curse" (V.x.28–29). They exit fighting.

SUMMARY: ACT V, SCENE XI
Malcolm and Siward walk together in the castle, which they have now effectively captured. Ross tells Siward that his son is dead. Macduff emerges with Macbeth's head in his hand and proclaims Malcolm King of Scotland. Malcolm declares that all his thanes will be made earls, according to the English system of peerage. They will be the first such lords in Scottish history. Cursing Macbeth and his "fiend-like" queen, Malcolm calls all those around him his friends and invites them all to see him crowned at Scone (V.xi.35).

ANALYSIS: ACT V, SCENES I–XI

The rapid tempo of the play's development accelerates into break-neck frenzy in Act V, as the relatively long scenes of previous acts are replaced by a flurry of short takes, each of which furthers the action toward its violent conclusion on the battlefield outside Dunsinane Castle. We see the army's and Malcolm's preparation for battle, the fulfillment of the witches' prophecies, and the demises of both Lady Macbeth and Macbeth. Lady Macbeth, her icy nerves shattered by the weight of guilt and paranoia, gives way to sleepwalking and a delusional belief that her hands are stained with blood. "Out, damned spot," she cries in one of the play's most famous lines, and adds, "[W]ho would have thought the old man to have had so much blood in him?" (V.i.30, 33–34). Her belief that nothing can wash away the blood is, of course, an ironic and painful reversal of her earlier claim to Macbeth that "[a] little water clears us of this deed" (II.ii.65). Macbeth, too, is unable to sleep. His and Lady Macbeth's sleeplessness was foreshadowed by Macbeth's hallucination at the moment of the murder, when he believed that a voice cried out "Macbeth does murder sleep" (II.ii.34).

Like Duncan's death and Macbeth's ascension to the kingship, Lady Macbeth's suicide does not take place onstage; it is merely reported. Macbeth seems numb in response to the news of his wife's death, which seems surprising, especially given the great love he appears to have borne for his wife. Yet, his indifferent response reflects the despair that has seized him as he realizes that what has come to seem the game of life is almost up. Indeed, Macbeth's speech following his wife's death is one of the most famous expressions of despair in all of literature. "Tomorrow, and tomorrow, and tomorrow," he says grimly,

> *Creeps in this petty pace from day to day*
> *To the last syllable of recorded time,*
> *And all our yesterdays have lighted fools*
> *The way to dusty death. Out, out brief candle.*
> *Life's but a walking shadow, a poor player*
> *That struts and frets his hour upon the stage,*
> *And then is heard no more. It is a tale*
> *Told by an idiot, full of sound and fury,*
> *Signifying nothing.*　　　　　　*(V.v.18–27)*

These words reflect Macbeth's feeling of hopelessness, of course, but they have a self-justifying streak as well—for if life is "full of sound and fury, / Signifying nothing," then Macbeth's crimes, too, are meaningless rather than evil.

Additionally, the speech's insistence that "[l]ife's . . . a poor player / That struts and frets his hour upon the stage" can be read as a dark and somewhat subversive commentary on the relationship between the audience and the play. After all, Macbeth *is* just a player on an English stage, and his statement undercuts the suspension of disbelief that the audience must maintain in order to enter the action of the play. If we take Macbeth's statement as expressing Shakespeare's own perspective on the theater, then the entire play can be seen as being "full of sound and fury, / Signifying nothing." Admittedly, it seems unlikely that the playwright would have put his own perspective on the stage in the mouth of a despairing, desperate murderer. Still, Macbeth's words remind us of the essential theatricality of the action—that the lengthy soliloquies, offstage deaths, and poetic speeches are not meant to capture reality but to reinterpret it in order to evoke a certain emotional response from the audience.

Despite the pure nihilism of this speech, Macbeth seems to fluctuate between despair and ridiculous bravado, making his own dissolution rougher and more complex than that of his wife. Lured into a false sense of security by the final prophecies of the witches, he gives way to boastfulness and a kind of self-destructive arrogance. When the battle begins, Macbeth clings, against all apparent evidence, to the notion that he will not be harmed because he is protected by the prophecy—although whether he really believes it at this stage, or is merely hanging on to the last thread of hope he has left, is debatable.

Macbeth ceased to be a sympathetic hero once he made the decision to kill Duncan, but by the end of the play he has become so morally repulsive that his death comes as a powerful relief. Ambition and bloodlust must be checked by virtue for order and form to be restored to the sound and fury of human existence. Only with Malcolm's victory and assumption of the crown can Scotland, and the play itself, be saved from the chaos engendered by Macbeth.

Important Quotations Explained

1. The raven himself is hoarse
    That croaks the fatal entrance of Duncan
    Under my battlements. Come, you spirits
    That tend on mortal thoughts, unsex me here,
    And fill me from the crown to the toe top-full
    Of direst cruelty. Make thick my blood,
    Stop up th'access and passage to remorse,
    That no compunctious visitings of nature
    Shake my fell purpose, nor keep peace between
    Th' effect and it. Come to my woman's breasts,
    And take my milk for gall, you murd'ring ministers,
    Wherever in your sightless substances
    You wait on nature's mischief. Come, thick night,
    And pall thee in the dunnest smoke of hell,
    That my keen knife see not the wound it makes,
    Nor heaven peep through the blanket of the dark,
    To cry 'Hold, hold!'

Lady Macbeth speaks these words in Act I, scene v, lines 36–52, as she awaits the arrival of King Duncan at her castle. We have previously seen Macbeth's uncertainty about whether he should take the crown by killing Duncan. In this speech, there is no such confusion, as Lady Macbeth is clearly willing to do whatever is necessary to seize the throne. Her strength of purpose is contrasted with her husband's tendency to waver. This speech shows the audience that Lady Macbeth is the real steel behind Macbeth and that her ambition will be strong enough to drive her husband forward. At the same time, the language of this speech touches on the theme of masculinity— "unsex me here / . . . / . . . Come to my woman's breasts, / And take my milk for gall," Lady Macbeth says as she prepares herself to commit murder. The language suggests that her womanhood, represented by breasts and milk, usually symbols of nurture, impedes her from performing acts of violence and cruelty, which she associates with manliness. Later, this sense of the relationship between masculinity and violence will be deepened when Macbeth is unwilling to go through with the murders and his wife tells him, in effect, that he needs to "be a man" and get on with it.

2.   If it were done when 'tis done, then 'twere well
        It were done quickly. If th'assassination
        Could trammel up the consequence, and catch
        With his surcease success: that but this blow
        Might be the be-all and the end-all, here,
        But here upon this bank and shoal of time,
        We'd jump the life to come. But in these cases
        We still have judgement here, that we but teach
        Bloody instructions which, being taught, return
        To plague th'inventor. This even-handed justice
        Commends th'ingredience of our poisoned chalice
        To our own lips. He's here in double trust:
        First, as I am his kinsman and his subject,
        Strong both against the deed; then, as his host,
        Who should against his murderer shut the door,
        Not bear the knife myself. Besides, this Duncan
        Hath borne his faculties so meek, hath been
        So clear in his great office, that his virtues
        Will plead like angels, trumpet-tongued against
        The deep damnation of his taking-off,
        And pity, like a naked new-born babe,
        Striding the blast, or heaven's cherubin, horsed
        Upon the sightless couriers of the air,
        Shall blow the horrid deed in every eye
        That tears shall drown the wind. I have no spur
        To prick the sides of my intent, but only
        Vaulting ambition which o'erleaps itself
        And falls on th'other.

In this soliloquy, which is found in Act I, scene vii, lines 1–28, Macbeth debates whether he should kill Duncan. When he lists Duncan's noble qualities (he "[h]ath borne his faculties so meek") and the loyalty that he feels toward his king ("I am his kinsman and his subject"), we are reminded of just how grave an outrage it is for the couple to slaughter their ruler while he is a guest in their house. At the same time, Macbeth's fear that "[w]e still have judgement here, that we but teach / Bloody instructions which, being taught, return / To plague th'inventor," foreshadows the way that his deeds will eventually come back to haunt him. The imagery in this speech is dark—we hear of "bloody instructions," "deep damnation," and a "poisoned chalice"—and suggests that Macbeth is aware of how the murder would open the door to a dark and sinful world. At the same time, he admits that his only reason for committing murder, "ambition," suddenly seems an insufficient justification for the act. The destruction that comes from unchecked ambition will continue to be explored as one of the play's themes. As the soliloquy ends, Macbeth seems to resolve not to kill Duncan, but this resolve will only last until his wife returns and once again convinces him, by the strength of her will, to go ahead with their plot.

3.   Whence is that knocking?—
       How is't with me, when every noise appals me?
       What hands are here! Ha, they pluck out mine eyes.
       Will all great Neptune's ocean wash this blood
       Clean from my hand? No, this my hand will rather
       The multitudinous seas incarnadine,
       Making the green one red.

Macbeth says this in Act II, scene ii, lines 55–61. He has just murdered Duncan, and the crime was accompanied by supernatural portents. Now he hears a mysterious knocking on his gate, which seems to promise doom. (In fact, the person knocking is Macduff, who will indeed eventually destroy Macbeth.) The enormity of Macbeth's crime has awakened in him a powerful sense of guilt that will hound him throughout the play. Blood, specifically Duncan's blood, serves as the symbol of that guilt, and Macbeth's sense that "all great Neptune's ocean" cannot cleanse him—that there is enough blood on his hands to turn the entire sea red—will stay with him until his death. Lady Macbeth's response to this speech will be her prosaic remark, "A little water clears us of this deed" (II.ii.65). By the end of the play, however, she will share Macbeth's sense that Duncan's murder has irreparably stained them with blood.

QUOTATIONS

4.   Out, damned spot; out, I say. One, two,—why, then 'tis
      time to do't. Hell is murky. Fie, my lord, fie, a soldier and
      afeard? What need we fear who knows it when none can
      call our power to account? Yet who would have thought
      the old man to have had so much blood in him?

These words are spoken by Lady Macbeth in Act V, scene i, lines
30–34, as she sleepwalks through Macbeth's castle on the eve of his
battle against Macduff and Malcolm. Earlier in the play, she pos-
sessed a stronger resolve and sense of purpose than her husband
and was the driving force behind their plot to kill Duncan. When
Macbeth believed his hand was irreversibly bloodstained earlier
in the play, Lady Macbeth had told him, "A little water clears us
of this deed" (II.ii.65). Now, however, she too sees blood. She is
completely undone by guilt and descends into madness. It may be a
reflection of her mental and emotional state that she is not speaking
in verse; this is one of the few moments in the play when a major
character—save for the witches, who speak in four-foot couplets—
strays from iambic pentameter. Her inability to sleep was foreshadowed in the voice that her husband thought he heard while killing
the king—a voice crying out that Macbeth was murdering sleep.
And her delusion that there is a bloodstain on her hand furthers
the play's use of blood as a symbol of guilt. "What need we fear
who knows it when none can call our power to account?" she asks,
asserting that as long as her and her husband's power is secure, the
murders they committed cannot harm them. But her guilt-racked
state and her mounting madness show how hollow her words are.
So, too, does the army outside her castle. "Hell is murky," she says,
implying that she already knows that darkness intimately. The pair,
in their destructive power, have created their own hell, where they
are tormented by guilt and insanity.

QUOTATIONS

5. She should have died hereafter.
   There would have been a time for such a word.
   Tomorrow, and tomorrow, and tomorrow
   Creeps in this petty pace from day to day
   To the last syllable of recorded time.
   And all our yesterdays have lighted fools
   The way to dusty death. Out, out, brief candle.
   Life's but a walking shadow, a poor player
   That struts and frets his hour upon the stage,
   And then is heard no more. It is a tale
   Told by an idiot, full of sound and fury,
   Signifying nothing.

These words are uttered by Macbeth after he hears of Lady Macbeth's death, in Act V, scene v, lines 16–27. Given the great love between them, his response is oddly muted, but it segues quickly into a speech of such pessimism and despair—one of the most famous speeches in all of Shakespeare—that the audience realizes how completely his wife's passing and the ruin of his power have undone Macbeth. His speech insists that there is no meaning or purpose in life. Rather, life "is a tale / Told by an idiot, full of sound and fury, / Signifying nothing." One can easily understand how, with his wife dead and armies marching against him, Macbeth succumbs to such pessimism. Yet, there is also a defensive and self-justifying quality to his words. If everything is meaningless, then Macbeth's awful crimes are somehow made less awful, because, like everything else, they too "signify nothing."

Macbeth's statement that "[l]ife's but a poor player / That struts and frets his hour upon the stage" can be read as Shakespeare's somewhat deflating reminder of the illusionary nature of the theater. After all, Macbeth is only a "player" himself, strutting on an Elizabethan stage. In any play, there is a conspiracy of sorts between the audience and the actors, as both pretend to accept the play's reality. Macbeth's comment calls attention to this conspiracy and partially explodes it—his nihilism embraces not only his own life but the entire play. If we take his words to heart, the play, too, can be seen as an event "full of sound and fury, / Signifying nothing."

KEY FACTS

FULL TITLE
The Tragedy of Macbeth

AUTHOR
William Shakespeare

TYPE OF WORK
Play

GENRE
Tragedy

LANGUAGE
English

TIME AND PLACE WRITTEN
1606, England

DATE OF FIRST PUBLICATION
First Folio edition, 1623

PUBLISHER
John Heminges and Henry Condell, two senior members of
Shakespeare's theatrical company

TONE
Dark and ominous, suggestive of a world turned topsy-turvy by
foul and unnatural crimes

TENSE
Not applicable (drama)

SETTING (TIME)
The Middle Ages, specifically the eleventh century

SETTING (PLACE)
Various locations in Scotland; also England, briefly

PROTAGONIST
Macbeth

MAJOR CONFLICTS

The struggle within Macbeth between his ambition and his sense of right and wrong; the struggle between the murderous evil represented by Macbeth and Lady Macbeth and the best interests of the nation, represented by Malcolm and Macduff

RISING ACTION

Macbeth and Banquo's encounter with the witches initiates both conflicts; Lady Macbeth's speeches goad Macbeth into murdering Duncan and seizing the crown.

CLIMAX

Macbeth's murder of Duncan in Act II represents the point of no return, after which Macbeth is forced to continue butchering his subjects to avoid the consequences of his crime.

FALLING ACTION

Macbeth's increasingly brutal murders (of Duncan's servants, Banquo, Lady Macduff and her son); Macbeth's second meeting with the witches; Macbeth's final confrontation with Macduff and the opposing armies

THEMES

The corrupting nature of unchecked ambition; the relationship between cruelty and masculinity; the difference between kingship and tyranny

MOTIFS

The supernatural, hallucinations, violence, prophecy

SYMBOLS

Blood; the dagger that Macbeth sees just before he kills Duncan in Act II; the weather

FORESHADOWING

The bloody battle in Act I foreshadows the bloody murders later on; when Macbeth thinks he hears a voice while killing Duncan, it foreshadows the insomnia that plagues Macbeth and his wife; Macduff's suspicions of Macbeth after Duncan's murder foreshadow his later opposition to Macbeth; all of the witches' prophecies foreshadow later events.

KEY FACTS

STUDY QUESTIONS

1. *Characterize the relationship between Macbeth and Lady Macbeth. If the main theme of* MACBETH *is ambition, whose ambition is the driving force of the play—Macbeth's, Lady Macbeth's, or both?*

The Macbeths' marriage, like the couple themselves, is atypical, particularly by the standards of its time. Yet despite their odd power dynamic, the two of them seem surprisingly attached to one another, particularly compared to other married couples in Shakespeare's plays, in which romantic felicity appears primarily during courtship and marriages tend to be troubled. Macbeth offers an exception to this rule, as Macbeth and his wife are partners in the truest sense of the word. Of course, the irony of their "happy" marriage is clear— they are united by their crimes, their mutual madness, and their mounting alienation from the rest of humanity.

Though Macbeth is a brave general and a powerful lord, his wife is far from subordinate to his will. Indeed, she often seems to control him, either by crafty manipulation or by direct order. And it is Lady Macbeth's deep-seated ambition, rather than her husband's, that ultimately propels the plot of the play by goading Macbeth to murder Duncan. Macbeth does not need any help coming up with the idea of murdering Duncan, but it seems unlikely that he would have committed the murder without his wife's powerful taunts and persuasions.

2. *One of the important themes in* MACBETH *is the idea of political legitimacy, of the moral authority that some kings possess and others lack. With particular attention to Malcolm's questioning of Macduff in Act IV, scene iii, try to define some of the characteristics that grant or invalidate the moral legitimacy of absolute power. What makes Duncan a good king? What makes Macbeth a tyrant?*

After Duncan's death, the nobles of Scotland begin to grumble among themselves about what they perceive as Macbeth's tyrannical behavior. When Macduff meets Malcolm in England, Malcolm pretends that he would make an even worse king than Macbeth in order to test Macduff's loyalty to Scotland. The bad qualities he claims to possess include lust, greed, and a chaotic and violent temperament. These qualities all seem characteristic of Macbeth, whereas Duncan's universally lauded reign was marked by the king's kindness, generosity, and stabilizing presence. The king must be able to keep order and should reward his subjects according to their merits. For example, Duncan makes Macbeth thane of Cawdor after Macbeth's victory over the invaders. Perhaps the most important quality of a true king to emerge in Malcolm's conversation with Macduff is loyalty to Scotland and its people above oneself. Macbeth wishes to be king to gratify his own desires, while Duncan and Malcolm wear the crown out of love for their nation.

3.   *An important theme in* MACBETH *is the relationship*
      between gender and power, particularly Shakespeare's
      exploration of the values that make up the idea of
      masculinity. What are these values, and how do various
      characters embody them? How does Shakespeare
      subvert his characters' perception of gender roles?

Manhood, for most of the characters in Macbeth, is tied to ideals of strength, power, physical courage, and force of will; it is rarely tied to ideals of intelligence or moral fortitude. At several points in the play, the characters goad one another into action by questioning each other's manhood. Most significantly, Lady Macbeth emasculates her husband repeatedly, knowing that in his desperation to prove his manhood he will perform the acts she wishes him to perform. Macbeth echoes Lady Macbeth's words when he questions the manhood of the murderers he has hired to kill Banquo, and after Macduff's wife and children are killed, Malcolm urges Macduff to take the news with manly reserve and to devote himself to the destruction of Macbeth, his family's murderer. Ultimately, there is a strong suggestion that manhood is tied to cruelty and violence: note Lady Macbeth's speech in Act I, scene v, when she asks to be "unsexed" so that she can help her husband commit murder. Yet, at the same time, the audience is clearly meant to realize that women provide the push that sets the bloody action of the play in motion. Macduff, too, suggests that the equation of masculinity with cruelty is not quite correct. His comments show that he believes emotion and reflection are also important attributes of the true man.

HOW TO WRITE
LITERARY ANALYSIS

THE LITERARY ESSAY: A STEP-BY-STEP GUIDE

When you read for pleasure, your only goal is enjoyment. You might find yourself reading to get caught up in an exciting story, to learn about an interesting time or place, or just to pass time. Maybe you're looking for inspiration, guidance, or a reflection of your own life. There are as many different, valid ways of reading a book as there are books in the world.

When you read a work of literature in an English class, however, you're being asked to read in a special way: you're being asked to perform *literary analysis*. To analyze something means to break it down into smaller parts and then examine how those parts work, both individually and together. Literary analysis involves examining all the parts of a novel, play, short story, or poem—elements such as character, setting, tone, and imagery—and thinking about how the author uses those elements to create certain effects.

A literary essay isn't a book review: you're not being asked whether or not you liked a book or whether you'd recommend it to another reader. A literary essay also isn't like the kind of book report you wrote when you were younger, where your teacher wanted you to summarize the book's action. A high school- or college-level literary essay asks, "How does this piece of literature actually work?" "How does it do what it does?" and, "Why might the author have made the choices he or she did?"

THE SEVEN STEPS
No one is born knowing how to analyze literature; it's a skill you learn and a process you can master. As you gain more practice with this kind of thinking and writing, you'll be able to craft a method that works best for you. But until then, here are seven basic steps to writing a well-constructed literary essay:

1. *Ask questions*
2. *Collect evidence*
3. *Construct a thesis*

4. *Develop and organize arguments*
5. *Write the introduction*
6. *Write the body paragraphs*
7. *Write the conclusion*

---

1. ASK QUESTIONS

When you're assigned a literary essay in class, your teacher will often provide you with a list of writing prompts. Lucky you! Now all you have to do is choose one. Do yourself a favor and pick a topic that interests you. You'll have a much better (not to mention easier) time if you start off with something you enjoy thinking about. If you are asked to come up with a topic by yourself, though, you might start to feel a little panicked. Maybe you have too many ideas—or none at all. Don't worry. Take a deep breath and start by asking yourself these questions:

- **What struck you?** Did a particular image, line, or scene linger in your mind for a long time? If it fascinated you, chances are you can draw on it to write a fascinating essay.

- **What confused you?** Maybe you were surprised to see a character act in a certain way, or maybe you didn't understand why the book ended the way it did. Confusing moments in a work of literature are like a loose thread in a sweater: if you pull on it, you can unravel the entire thing. Ask yourself why the author chose to write about that character or scene the way he or she did and you might tap into some important insights about the work as a whole.

- **Did you notice any patterns?** Is there a phrase that the main character uses constantly or an image that repeats throughout the book? If you can figure out how that pattern weaves through the work and what the significance of that pattern is, you've almost got your entire essay mapped out.

- **Did you notice any contradictions or ironies?** Great works of literature are complex; great literary essays recognize and explain those complexities. Maybe the title (*Happy Days*) totally disagrees with the book's subject matter (hungry orphans dying in the woods). Maybe the main character acts one way around his family and a completely different way around his friends and associates. If you can find a way to explain a work's contradictory elements, you've got the seeds of a great essay.

At this point, you don't need to know exactly what you're going to say about your topic; you just need a place to begin your exploration. You can help direct your reading and brainstorming by formulating your topic as a *question,* which you'll then try to answer in your essay. The best questions invite critical debates and discussions, not just a rehashing of the summary. Remember, you're looking for something you can *prove or argue* based on evidence you find in the text. Finally, remember to keep the scope of your question in mind: is this a topic you can adequately address within the word or page limit you've been given? Conversely, is this a topic big enough to fill the required length?

GOOD QUESTIONS

"Are Romeo and Juliet's parents responsible for the deaths of their children?"

"Why do pigs keep showing up in LORD OF THE FLIES*?"*

"Are Dr. Frankenstein and his monster alike? How?"

BAD QUESTIONS

"What happens to Scout in TO KILL A MOCKINGBIRD*?"*

"What do the other characters in JULIUS CAESAR *think about Caesar?"*

"How does Hester Prynne in THE SCARLET LETTER *remind me of my sister?"*

---

2. COLLECT EVIDENCE

Once you know what question you want to answer, it's time to scour the book for things that will help you answer the question. Don't worry if you don't know what you want to say yet—right now you're just collecting ideas and material and letting it all percolate. Keep track of passages, symbols, images, or scenes that deal with your topic. Eventually, you'll start making connections between these examples and your thesis will emerge.

Here's a brief summary of the various parts that compose each and every work of literature. These are the elements that you will analyze in your essay, and which you will offer as evidence to support your arguments. For more on the parts of literary works, see the Glossary of Literary Terms at the end of this section.

ELEMENTS OF STORY   These are the *what*s of the work—what happens, where it happens, and to whom it happens.

- **Plot:** All of the events and actions of the work.

- **Character:** The people who act and are acted upon in a literary work. The main character of a work is known as the *protagonist.*

- **Conflict:** The central tension in the work. In most cases, the protagonist wants something, while opposing forces (antagonists) hinder the protagonist's progress.

- **Setting:** When and where the work takes place. Elements of setting include location, time period, time of day, weather, social atmosphere, and economic conditions.

- **Narrator:** The person telling the story. The narrator may straightforwardly report what happens, convey the subjective opinions and perceptions of one or more characters, or provide commentary and opinion in his or her own voice.

- **Themes:** The main idea or message of the work—usually an abstract idea about people, society, or life in general. A work may have many themes, which may be in tension with one another.

ELEMENTS OF STYLE   These are the *how*s—how the characters speak, how the story is constructed, and how language is used throughout the work.

- **Structure and organization:** How the parts of the work are assembled. Some novels are narrated in a linear, chronological fashion, while others skip around in time. Some plays follow a traditional three- or five-act structure, while others are a series of loosely connected scenes. Some authors deliberately leave gaps in their works, leaving readers to puzzle out the missing information. A work's structure and organization can tell you a lot about the kind of message it wants to convey.

- **Point of view:** The perspective from which a story is told. In *first-person point of view*, the narrator involves him or herself in the story. ("I went to the store"; "We watched in horror as the bird slammed into the window.") A first-person narrator is usually the protagonist of the work, but not always. In *third-person point of view*, the narrator does not participate in the story. A third-person narrator may closely follow a specific character, recounting that individual character's thoughts or experiences, or it may be what we call an *omniscient* narrator. Omniscient narrators see and know all: they can witness any event in any time or place and are privy to the inner thoughts and feelings of all characters. Remember that the narrator and the author are not the same thing!

- **Diction:** Word choice. Whether a character uses dry, clinical language or flowery prose with lots of exclamation points can tell you a lot about his or her attitude and personality.

- **Syntax:** Word order and sentence construction. Syntax is a crucial part of establishing an author's narrative voice. Ernest Hemingway, for example, is known for writing in very short, straightforward sentences, while James Joyce characteristically wrote in long, incredibly complicated lines.

- **Tone:** The mood or feeling of the text. Diction and syntax often contribute to the tone of a work. A novel written in short, clipped sentences that use small, simple words might feel brusque, cold, or matter-of-fact.

- **Imagery:** Language that appeals to the senses, representing things that can be seen, smelled, heard, tasted, or touched.

- **Figurative language:** Language that is not meant to be interpreted literally. The most common types of figurative language are *metaphors* and *similes,* which compare two unlike things in order to suggest a similarity between them— for example, "All the world's a stage," or "The moon is like a ball of green cheese." (Metaphors say one thing *is* another thing; similes claim that one thing is *like* another thing.)

---

3. CONSTRUCT A THESIS

When you've examined all the evidence you've collected and know how you want to answer the question, it's time to write your thesis statement. A *thesis* is a claim about a work of literature that needs to be supported by evidence and arguments. The thesis statement is the heart of the literary essay, and the bulk of your paper will be spent trying to prove this claim. A good thesis will be:

- **Arguable.** "*The Great Gatsby* describes New York society in the 1920s" isn't a thesis—it's a fact.

- **Provable through textual evidence.** "*Hamlet* is a confusing but ultimately very well-written play" is a weak thesis because it offers the writer's personal opinion about the book. Yes, it's arguable, but it's not a claim that can be proved or supported with examples taken from the play itself.

- **Surprising.** "Both George and Lenny change a great deal in *Of Mice and Men*" is a weak thesis because it's obvious. A really strong thesis will argue for a reading of the text that is not immediately apparent.

- **Specific.** "Dr. Frankenstein's monster tells us a lot about the human condition" is *almost* a really great thesis statement, but it's still too vague. What does the writer mean by "a lot"? *How* does the monster tell us so much about the human condition?

GOOD THESIS STATEMENTS

Question: In *Romeo and Juliet*, which is more powerful in shaping the lovers' story: fate or foolishness?

Thesis: "Though Shakespeare defines Romeo and Juliet as 'star-crossed lovers' and images of stars and planets appear throughout the play, a closer examination of that celestial imagery reveals that the stars are merely witnesses to the characters' foolish activities and not the causes themselves."

Question: How does the bell jar function as a symbol in Sylvia Plath's *The Bell Jar*?

Thesis: "A bell jar is a bell-shaped glass that has three basic uses: to hold a specimen for observation, to contain gases, and to maintain a vacuum. The bell jar appears in each of these capacities in *The Bell Jar*, Plath's semi-autobiographical novel, and each appearances marks a different stage in Esther's mental breakdown."

Question: Would Piggy in *The Lord of the Flies* make a good island leader if he were given the chance?

Thesis: "Though the intelligent, rational, and innovative Piggy has the mental characteristics of a good leader, he ultimately lacks the social skills necessary to be an effective one. Golding emphasizes this point by giving Piggy a foil in the charismatic Jack, whose magnetic personality allows him to capture and wield power effectively, if not always wisely."

4. Develop and Organize Arguments

The reasons and examples that support your thesis will form the middle paragraphs of your essay. Since you can't really write your thesis statement until you know how you'll structure your argument, you'll probably end up working on steps 3 and 4 at the same time.

There's no single method of argumentation that will work in every context. One essay prompt might ask you to compare and contrast two characters, while another asks you to trace an image through a given work of literature. These questions require different kinds of answers and therefore different kinds of arguments. Below, we'll discuss three common kinds of essay prompts and some strategies for constructing a solid, well-argued case.

Types of Literary Essays

- **Compare and contrast**

  Compare and contrast the characters of Huck and Jim in The Adventures of Huckleberry Finn.

  Chances are you've written this kind of essay before. In an academic literary context, you'll organize your arguments the same way you would in any other class. You can either go *subject by subject* or *point by point*. In the former, you'll discuss one character first and then the second. In the latter, you'll choose several traits (attitude toward life, social status, images and metaphors associated with the character) and devote a paragraph to each. You may want to use a mix of these two approaches—for example, you may want to spend a paragraph a piece broadly sketching Huck's and Jim's personalities before transitioning into a paragraph or two that describes a few key points of comparison. This can be a highly effective strategy if you want to make a counterintuitive argument—that, despite seeming to be totally different, the two objects being compared are actually similar in a very important way (or vice versa). Remember that your essay should reveal something fresh or unexpected about the text, so think beyond the obvious parallels and differences.

- **Trace**

  Choose an image—for example, birds, knives, or eyes—and trace that image throughout Macbeth.

  Sounds pretty easy, right? All you need to do is read the play, underline every appearance of a knife in *Macbeth,* and then list them in your essay in the order they appear, right? Well, not exactly. Your teacher doesn't want a simple catalog of examples. He or she wants to see you make *connections* between those examples—that's the difference between summarizing and analyzing. In the *Macbeth* example above, think about the different contexts in which knives appear in the play and to what effect. In *Macbeth*, there are real knives and imagined knives; knives that kill and knives that simply threaten. Categorize and classify your examples to give them some order. Finally, always keep the overall effect in mind. After you choose and analyze your examples, you should come to some greater understanding about the work, as well as your chosen image, symbol, or phrase's role in developing the major themes and stylistic strategies of that work.

- **Debate**

  Is the society depicted in 1984 *good for its citizens?*

In this kind of essay, you're being asked to debate a moral, ethical, or aesthetic issue regarding the work. You might be asked to judge a character or group of characters (*Is Caesar responsible for his own demise?*) or the work itself (*Is* JANE EYRE *a feminist novel?*). For this kind of essay, there are two important points to keep in mind. First, don't simply base your arguments on your personal feelings and reactions. Every literary essay expects you to read and analyze the work, so search for evidence in the text. What do characters in *1984* have to say about the government of Oceania? What images does Orwell use that might give you a hint about his attitude toward the government? As in any debate, you also need to make sure that you define all the necessary terms before you begin to argue your case. What does it mean to be a "good" society? What makes a novel "feminist"? You should define your terms right up front, in the first paragraph after your introduction.

Second, remember that strong literary essays make contrary and surprising arguments. Try to think outside the box. In the *1984* example above, it seems like the obvious answer would be no, the totalitarian society depicted in Orwell's novel is *not* good for its citizens. But can you think of any arguments for the opposite side? Even if your final assertion is that the novel depicts a cruel, repressive, and therefore harmful society, acknowledging and responding to the counterargument will strengthen your overall case.

5. WRITE THE INTRODUCTION

Your introduction sets up the entire essay. It's where you present your topic and articulate the particular issues and questions you'll be addressing. It's also where you, as the writer, introduce yourself to your readers. A persuasive literary essay immediately establishes its writer as a knowledgeable, authoritative figure.

An introduction can vary in length depending on the overall length of the essay, but in a traditional five-paragraph essay it should be no longer than one paragraph. However long it is, your introduction needs to:

- **Provide any necessary context.** Your introduction should situate the reader and let him or her know what to expect. What book are you discussing? Which characters? What topic will you be addressing?

- **Answer the "So what?" question.** Why is this topic important, and why is your particular position on the topic noteworthy? Ideally, your introduction should pique the reader's interest by suggesting how your argument is surprising or otherwise counterintuitive. Literary essays make unexpected connections and reveal less-than-obvious truths.

- **Present your thesis.** This usually happens at or very near the end of your introduction.

- **Indicate the shape of the essay to come.** Your reader should finish reading your introduction with a good sense of the scope of your essay as well as the path you'll take toward proving your thesis. You don't need to spell out every step, but you do need to suggest the organizational pattern you'll be using.

Your introduction should not:

- **Be vague.** Beware of the two killer words in literary analysis: *interesting* and *important*. Of course the work, question, or example is interesting and important—that's why you're writing about it!

- **Open with any grandiose assertions.** Many student readers think that beginning their essays with a flamboyant statement such as, "Since the dawn of time, writers have been fascinated with the topic of free will," makes them sound important and commanding. You know what? It actually sounds pretty amateurish.

- **Wildly praise the work.** Another typical mistake student writers make is extolling the work or author. Your teacher doesn't need to be told that "Shakespeare is perhaps the greatest writer in the English language." You can mention a work's reputation in passing—by referring to *The Adventures of Huckleberry Finn* as "Mark Twain's enduring classic," for example—but don't make a point of bringing it up unless that reputation is key to your argument.

- **Go off-topic.** Keep your introduction streamlined and to the point. Don't feel the need to throw in all kinds of bells and whistles in order to impress your reader—just get to the point as quickly as you can, without skimping on any of the required steps.

6. WRITE THE BODY PARAGRAPHS

Once you've written your introduction, you'll take the arguments you developed in step 4 and turn them into your body paragraphs. The organization of this middle section of your essay will largely be determined by the argumentative strategy you use, but no matter how you arrange your thoughts, your body paragraphs need to do the following:

- **Begin with a strong topic sentence.** Topic sentences are like signs on a highway: they tell the reader where they are and where they're going. A good topic sentence not only alerts readers to what issue will be discussed in the following paragraph but also gives them a sense of what argument will be made *about* that issue. "Rumor and gossip play an important role in *The Crucible*" isn't a strong topic sentence because it doesn't tell us very much. "The community's constant gossiping creates an environment that allows false accusations to flourish" is a much stronger topic sentence— it not only tells us *what* the paragraph will discuss (gossip) but *how* the paragraph will discuss the topic (by showing how gossip creates a set of conditions that leads to the play's climactic action).

- **Fully and completely develop a single thought.** Don't skip around in your paragraph or try to stuff in too much material. Body paragraphs are like bricks: each individual

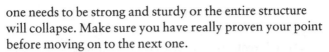

one needs to be strong and sturdy or the entire structure will collapse. Make sure you have really proven your point before moving on to the next one.

- **Use transitions effectively.** Good literary essay writers know that each paragraph must be clearly and strongly linked to the material around it. Think of each paragraph as a response to the one that precedes it. Use transition words and phrases such as *however, similarly, on the contrary, therefore,* and *furthermore* to indicate what kind of response you're making.

---

7. WRITE THE CONCLUSION

Just as you used the introduction to ground your readers in the topic before providing your thesis, you'll use the conclusion to quickly summarize the specifics learned thus far and then hint at the broader implications of your topic. A good conclusion will:

- **Do more than simply restate the thesis.** If your thesis argued that *The Catcher in the Rye* can be read as a Christian allegory, don't simply end your essay by saying, "And that is why *The Catcher in the Rye* can be read as a Christian allegory." If you've constructed your arguments well, this kind of statement will just be redundant.

- **Synthesize the arguments, not summarize them.** Similarly, don't repeat the details of your body paragraphs in your conclusion. The reader has already read your essay, and chances are it's not so long that they've forgotten all your points by now.

- **Revisit the "So what?" question.** In your introduction, you made a case for why your topic and position are important. You should close your essay with the same sort of gesture. What do your readers know now that they didn't know before? How will that knowledge help them better appreciate or understand the work overall?

- **Move from the specific to the general.** Your essay has most likely treated a very specific element of the work—a single character, a small set of images, or a particular passage. In your conclusion, try to show how this narrow discussion has wider implications for the work overall. If your essay on *To Kill a Mockingbird* focused on the character of Boo Radley, for example, you might want to include a bit in your conclusion about how he fits into the novel's larger message about childhood, innocence, or family life.

- **Stay relevant.** Your conclusion should suggest new directions of thought, but it shouldn't be treated as an opportunity to pad your essay with all the extra, interesting ideas you came up with during your brainstorming sessions but couldn't fit into the essay proper. Don't attempt to stuff in unrelated queries or too many abstract thoughts.

- **Avoid making overblown closing statements.** A conclusion should open up your highly specific, focused discussion, but it should do so without drawing a sweeping lesson about life or human nature. Making such observations may be part of the point of reading, but it's almost always a mistake in essays, where these observations tend to sound overly dramatic or simply silly.

A+ Essay Checklist

Congratulations! If you've followed all the steps we've outlined above, you should have a solid literary essay to show for all your efforts. What if you've got your sights set on an A+? To write the kind of superlative essay that will be rewarded with a perfect grade, keep the following rubric in mind. These are the qualities that teachers expect to see in a truly A+ essay. How does yours stack up?

- ✓ Demonstrates a thorough understanding of the book
- ✓ Presents an original, compelling argument
- ✓ Thoughtfully analyzes the text's formal elements
- ✓ Uses appropriate and insightful examples
- ✓ Structures ideas in a logical and progressive order
- ✓ Demonstrates a mastery of sentence construction, transitions, grammar, spelling, and word choice

SUGGESTED ESSAY TOPICS

1. *The fantastical and grotesque witches are among the most memorable figures in the play. How does Shakespeare characterize the witches? What is their thematic significance?*

2. *Compare and contrast Macbeth, Macduff, and Banquo. How are they alike? How are they different? Is it possible to argue that Macbeth is the play's villain and Macduff or Banquo its hero, or is the matter more complicated than that?*

3. *Discuss the role that blood plays in* MACBETH, *particularly immediately following Duncan's murder and late in the play. What does it symbolize for Macbeth and his wife?*

4. *Discuss Macbeth's visions and hallucinations. What role do they play in the development of his character?*

5. *Is* MACBETH *a moral play? Is justice served at the end of the play? Defend your answer.*

6. *Discuss Shakespeare's use of the technique of elision, in which certain key events take place offstage. Why do you think he uses this technique?*

A+ STUDENT ESSAY

> Equivocation is the practice of deliberately deceiving
> a listener without explicitly lying, either by using
> ambiguously misleading language or by withholding
> crucial information. What is the significance of
> equivocation in *Macbeth*?

Macbeth is a play about subterfuge and trickery. Macbeth, his wife, and the three Weird Sisters are linked in their mutual refusal to come right out and say things directly. Instead, they rely on implications, riddles, and ambiguity to evade the truth. Macbeth's ability to manipulate his language and his public image in order to hide his foul crimes makes him a very modern-seeming politician. However, his inability to see past the witches' equivocations—even as he utilizes the practice himself—ultimately leads to his downfall.

Sometimes, equivocations in *Macbeth* are meant kindly, as when Ross tries to spare Macduff's feelings by telling him that his wife and son are "well." Macduff initially takes this to mean that his family is alive and healthy, but Ross means that they are dead and in heaven. More often than not, though, such ambiguous statements lead to harm. The witches' deceptive prophecies are perhaps the most destructive instances of equivocation. They tell Macbeth that he can never be harmed by anyone "of woman born," but they neglect to tell him that Macduff was surgically removed from his mother's womb and therefore doesn't fall into that category. Similarly, they tell Macbeth that he can't be defeated until Birnam Wood comes to Dunsinane, but they don't alert him to the possibility that the opposing army might advance on his castle under cover of branches cut from Birnam trees.

Macbeth ignores several signs that might have alerted him to the witches' deceptive capabilities. Banquo warns Macbeth to be wary of their predictions, since evil creatures will sometimes win people's confidence with "honest trifles"—small truths—only to betray them more deeply in the future. Indeed, the witches promise Macbeth fame and honor while withholding important information about the consequences that will follow. If Macbeth had been listening closely to the witches' language, he might have picked up on the their potential for trickery himself. The three Weird Sisters greet Banquo with a series of riddling titles, hailing him as "Lesser than

Macbeth, and greater" and "Not so happy, yet much happier." The phrases sound like nonsense, but in reality both assertions in each statement are true. Banquo will have a lesser title than Macbeth, but is the greater (i.e., more moral) man. He will not be as fortunate as Macbeth in the short term, as he will soon be assassinated, but will ultimately be much more fortunate because he won't be made to suffer the everlasting torments of hell. At no point do the witches lie to Macbeth—he simply hears what he wants to hear and ignores the rest.

It is ironic that Macbeth falls for the witches' equivocations, because Macbeth and his wife are master equivocators themselves. Duncan laments that there's no method with which one may find "the mind's construction in the face," meaning that it is impossible to know what a person is truly thinking just from his or her outward appearance. Lady Macbeth mimics this language when she directs her husband to look like an "innocent flower" in order to hide the "serpent" that truly lurks in his heart. The Macbeths know how to use imagery and appearance to conceal the truth, and sometimes they even use those skills on themselves. Macbeth asks the stars to extinguish their light so that his "eye" cannot see what his "hand" does. Similarly, Lady Macbeth asks the night to grow as dark as the "smoke of hell" so that her knife cannot see itself slash its victim. The Macbeths know that their acts are wicked, so they try to hide the knowledge of their deeds from their own consciousness. In a sense, they wish to equivocate to themselves.

Just before Macduff kills him, Macbeth swears that he will never again believe those "juggling fiends" that manipulate words and speak "in a double sense." However, it's possible that the three Weird Sisters are not "fiends," or demons, at all, but rather agents of morality who bring Macbeth to justice by trapping him with his own tricks. The drunken porter, imagining himself the keeper of hell's gates, pretends to admit "an equivocator that could swear in both the scales against either scale, who committed treason enough for God's sake, yet could not equivocate to heaven." One can imagine Macbeth receiving a similar welcome from the true porter of hell's gates.

GLOSSARY OF LITERARY TERMS

ANTAGONIST

The entity that acts to frustrate the goals of the *protagonist*. The antagonist is usually another *character* but may also be a non-human force.

ANTIHERO / ANTIHEROINE

A *protagonist* who is not admirable or who challenges notions of what should be considered admirable.

CHARACTER

A person, animal, or any other thing with a personality that appears in a *narrative*.

CLIMAX

The moment of greatest intensity in a text or the major turning point in the *plot*.

CONFLICT

The central struggle that moves the *plot* forward. The conflict can be the *protagonist*'s struggle against fate, nature, society, or another person.

FIRST-PERSON POINT OF VIEW

A literary style in which the *narrator* tells the story from his or her own *point of view* and refers to himself or herself as "I." The narrator may be an active participant in the story or just an observer.

HERO / HEROINE

The principal *character* in a literary work or *narrative*.

IMAGERY

Language that brings to mind sense-impressions, representing things that can be seen, smelled, heard, tasted, or touched.

MOTIF

A recurring idea, structure, contrast, or device that develops or informs the major *themes* of a work of literature.

NARRATIVE

A story.

NARRATOR

The person (sometimes a *character*) who tells a story; the *voice* assumed by the writer. The narrator and the author of the work of literature are not the same person.

PLOT

The arrangement of the events in a story, including the sequence in which they are told, the relative emphasis they are given, and the causal connections between events.

POINT OF VIEW

The *perspective* that a *narrative* takes toward the events it describes.

PROTAGONIST

The main *character* around whom the story revolves.

SETTING

The location of a *narrative* in time and space. Setting creates mood or atmosphere.

SUBPLOT

A secondary *plot* that is of less importance to the overall story but may serve as a point of contrast or comparison to the main plot.

SYMBOL

An object, *character*, figure, or color that is used to represent an abstract idea or concept. Unlike an *emblem,* a symbol may have different meanings in different contexts.

SYNTAX

The way the words in a piece of writing are put together to form lines, phrases, or clauses; the basic structure of a piece of writing.

THEME

A fundamental and universal idea explored in a literary work.

TONE

The author's attitude toward the subject or *characters* of a story or poem or toward the reader.

VOICE

An author's individual way of using language to reflect his or her own personality and attitudes. An author communicates voice through *tone, diction,* and *syntax.*

LITERARY ANALYSIS

A NOTE ON PLAGIARISM

Plagiarism—presenting someone else's work as your own—rears its ugly head in many forms. Many students know that copying text without citing it is unacceptable. But some don't realize that even if you're not quoting directly, but instead are paraphrasing or summarizing, *it is plagiarism* unless you cite the source.

Here are the most common forms of plagiarism:

- Using an author's phrases, sentences, or paragraphs without citing the source
- Paraphrasing an author's ideas without citing the source
- Passing off another student's work as your own

How do you steer clear of plagiarism? You should *always* acknowledge all words and ideas that aren't your own by using quotation marks around verbatim text or citations like footnotes and endnotes to note another writer's ideas. For more information on how to give credit when credit is due, ask your teacher for guidance or visit www.sparknotes.com.

Review & Resources

Quiz

1. Who kills Macbeth?

    A. Macduff
    B. Banquo
    C. Lady Macbeth
    D. Malcolm

2. How many men reign as king of Scotland throughout the play?

    A. 1
    B. 2
    C. 3
    D. 4

3. Whom does Lady Macbeth frame for the murder of Duncan?

    A. Malcolm and Donalbain
    B. Duncan's drunken chamberlains
    C. The porter
    D. Macbeth

4. Who kills Banquo?

    A. Macduff
    B. Fleance
    C. Macbeth
    D. A group of murderers hired by Macbeth

5. Which of the following best describes Lady Macbeth's death?

    A. She dies offstage.
    B. She sleepwalks off of the palace wall.
    C. She declares her own guilt and stabs herself with a knife.
    D. Macduff slays her in revenge for his own wife's murder.

6. Who discovers Duncan's body?

    A. Lennox
    B. Ross
    C. Macduff
    D. Donalbain

7. Whom does Macbeth see sitting in his chair during the banquet?

    A. himself
    B. Banquo's ghost
    C. Duncan's ghost
    D. Lady Macbeth

8. What vision does Macbeth have before he kills Duncan?

    A. He sees a floating head urging him to spill blood.
    B. He sees a bloody axe lodged in Duncan's brow.
    C. He sees a pale maiden weeping in the moonlight.
    D. He sees a floating dagger pointing him to Duncan's chamber.

9. With whom are the Scots at war at the beginning of the play?

    A. Norway
    B. Denmark
    C. Poland
    D. Finland

10. Which nation's army invades Scotland at the end of the play?

    A. Norway
    B. France
    C. England
    D. Finland

11. Who is the goddess of witchcraft in the play?

    A. Aphrodite
    B. Hecate
    C. Minerva
    D. Mordred

12. Who kills Donalbain?

    A.   Macbeth
    B.   Malcolm
    C.   A group of murderers hired by Macbeth
    D.   No one

13. What happens to Lady Macbeth before she dies?

    A.   She is plagued by fits of sleepwalking.
    B.   She is haunted by the ghost of Duncan.
    C.   She sees her children killed in battle.
    D.   She sees her children killed by Macbeth.

14. Who kills Lord Siward's son?

    A.   Duncan
    B.   Lennox
    C.   Macbeth
    D.   Ross

15. Where are Scottish kings crowned?

    A.   Edinburgh
    B.   Scone
    C.   London
    D.   Dunsinane

16. Why is Macduff able to kill Macbeth despite the witches' prophecy?

    A.   He kills the witches first.
    B.   He receives a charm from Grinswindle.
    C.   He is a powerful warlock himself.
    D.   He was born by cesarean section.

17. Where is Duncan killed?

    A.   In the battle with Norway
    B.   In his bedchamber at Macbeth's castle
    C.   In his bedchamber at Forres
    D.   At Birnam Wood

REVIEW & RESOURCES

18. Who flees Scotland to join Malcolm in England?

    A. Donalbain
    B. Ross
    C. Macduff
    D. Lennox

19. What was the weather like the night Duncan was murdered?

    A. Stormy and violent
    B. Calm and placid
    C. Foggy and ominous
    D. It was a night like any other night, according to
       Lennox

20. Who kills Lady Macbeth?

    A. Macbeth
    B. Macduff
    C. Lady Macduff
    D. Lady Macbeth

21. Who flees Scotland immediately after Duncan's death?

    A. Macbeth
    B. Malcolm and Donalbain
    C. Fleance
    D. Lennox

22. Who jokes that he works at "hell gate"?

    A. Macbeth
    B. Macduff
    C. The porter
    D. Duncan

23. What title is Macbeth given after his victory described in
    Act I?

    A. Thane of Cawdor
    B. Thane of Ross
    C. King of Scotland
    D. Prince of Cumberland

24. Who tells Macduff that his family has been killed?

    A. Donalbain
    B. Macbeth
    C. Lady Macduff
    D. Ross

25. How does Birnam Wood come to Dunsinane?

    A. By magic
    B. Through an earthquake
    C. It doesn't
    D. Malcolm's army hides behind cut-off tree branches

ANSWER KEY

1: A; 2: C; 3: B; 4: D; 5: A; 6: C; 7: B; 8: D; 9: A; 10: C; 11: B; 12: D;
13: A; 14: C; 15: B; 16: D; 17: B; 18: C; 19: C; 20: D; 21: B; 22: C;
23: A; 24: D; 25: D

SUGGESTIONS FOR FURTHER READING

BLOOM, HAROLD. *Shakespeare: The Invention of the Human.* New York: Riverhead Books, 1998.

BLOOM, HAROLD, ed. *Shakespeare's* MACBETH. New York: Riverhead Books, 2004.

BRADLEY, A. C. *Shakespearean Tragedy: Lectures on* HAMLET, OTHELLO, KING LEAR, & MACBETH. New York: Palgrave Macmillan, 2007.

HARBAGE, ALFRED. *William Shakespeare: A Reader's Guide.* New York: Octagon Books, 1971.

HAWKES, TERENCE, ed. *Twentieth-Century Interpretations of* MACBETH: *A Collection of Critical Essays.* Englewood Cliffs, NJ: Prentice-Hall, 1977.

MUIR, KENNETH. *Shakespeare's Tragic Sequence.* Oxford, UK: Routledge, reprint edition 2005.

SHAKESPEARE, WILLIAM. *The Norton Shakespeare.* Ed. Stephen Greenblatt. New York: W. W. Norton & Co., 1997.

SIEGEL, PAUL. *Shakespearean Tragedy and the Elizabethan Compromise.* New York: New York University Press, 1957.

REVIEW & RESOURCES